Virgin

T E R R I T O R Y

CATHY ALTER

STORIES FROM

THE ROAD

TO WOMANHOOD

Virgin

TERRITORY

THREE RIVERS PRESS · NEW YORK

Published by Three Rivers Press, New York, New York.
Member of the Crown Publishing Group, a division of Random House, Inc.
www.crownpublishing.com

THREE RIVERS PRESS and the Tugboat design are registered trademarks of Random House, Inc.

Printed in the United States of America

DESIGN BY ELINA D. NUDELMAN

Library of Congress Cataloging-in-Publication Data
Alter, Cathy.
Virgin territory : stories from the road to womanhood / Cathy Alter.—1st ed.
1. Teenage girls—Psychology.   2. Teenage girls—Conduct of life.   3. Adolescence.   4. Interpersonal relations in adolescence.   I. Title.
HQ798.A57   2004
305.235'2—dc22

2003017509

ISBN 1-4000-4781-1

10 9 8 7 6 5 4 3 2 1

First Edition

ALWAYS FOR MY PARENTS

acknowledgments

Without sounding too Grammy acceptance speech, I'd like to thank the following people, whose guidance, hand-holding, and supreme friendship I value more than gold:

My much-adored agent, Dan Mandel.

My super cool editor, Carrie Thornton, and everyone else who helped turn a bunch of words into a book: Camille Smith, Janet Biehl, Katherine Beitner, Elina Nudelman, Laura Duffy, and Linnea Knollmueller.

My (hopefully) discreet transcriber, Billy Fox, who now knows more about me than my therapist.

The dear men in my life who keep me on my toes: Matt, Dave, E.B., Marc, Karl, and my beloved brother, David. And to Otto, for giving me so many of my firsts.

The treasured women in my life who keep me sane: Bonita, Stacy, Libby, Corinna, Cari, Missy, Abby, and lifelong friends Gail and Amy.

Finally, I'd like to thank the women who participated in this book by opening their metaphorical diaries to a total stranger. I will be forever touched and grateful and inspired.

contents

PART II

Clearing a Path

CONTENTS

PART III
Branching Out

Foreword

BY JENNIFER WEINER

Ask a woman about her first time, and you're bound to get a story about sex—a seriocomic tale about a warm spring night in a boring Connecticut suburb, a few preparatory shots of Jägermeister, a pullout couch with a pancake-flat mattress, a little bit of pain, the faint rumor of pleasure, and a quick scoot home in the wee hours of the morning in case Mom thought to check up on the I'm-sleeping-over-at-Pam's-house excuse.

Or maybe that's just me.

The truth, as *Virgin Territory* so beautifully illustrates, is that every woman is the repository of dozens of first-time stories— some of them hilarious, some of them heartbreaking, all of them significant on that slick and winding, Jägermeister-scented road toward womanhood.

I can remember my first night away from home (a sleepover at Camp Shalom—I was so grossed out by the cabin's dingy, cob-webbed bathroom that I didn't pee for eighteen hours) and my first miniskirt (gray corduroy, eighth grade, Lord & Taylor in West Hartford).

I remember the first time I ate sushi and the first time I got drunk (because I grew up in the aforementioned boring Con-necticut suburb, the drunkening came well before the tekka maki).

I could tell you the story of the first time I fell in love and the first time I fell in love with someone who loved me back (they were not, alas, the same time).

But if I had to tell the story of my favorite first, it would be this one: the first time I was allowed to ride my bike the five miles to the Farmington Valley Mall, holding my breath as I pedaled alongside cars on busy streets, planting my feet on the pavement as I waited for a red light to change, riding carefully through the parking lot and padlocking my bike to the bike rack. It was October—a cool, crisp, sunny day. I had ten dollars of babysitting money in my pocket and my eye on a Star Trek novel and a bag of chocolate-covered pretzels. I was twelve years old and filled with a wonderful sense of freedom and exhilaration and the feel-ing of independence and even adulthood that goes along with being able to go where you want, when you want, under your own power.

I was twelve, too—and, if you haven't guessed, not particularly social—the first time I got completely lost in a book, swept away in its adventures, feeling like I knew the characters that peopled its pages better than I knew the sister who shared my bedroom. The book was *The Talisman* by Stephen King and Peter Straub, and I bought it in hardcover at that same mall and read it over a two-day stretch, guzzling it down in furious hot-eyed gulps. I remem-ber the same sense of freedom and exhilaration and power that my bike ride had given me: that sense that I could go anywhere, be anyone, take myself away from my real life and find a world that I liked better.

I remember thinking that the book was a kind of magic, and that being able to tell a story like that—being able to write something so thrilling, so gripping, so real—was a kind of magic, too; and wondering whether I'd be able to do it, whether I'd be brave enough to even try . . . and lying on the bed in a pool of light three hours past my bedtime and thinking, I will never forget how this feels.

There were good firsts and bad firsts after that—first heartbreak, first betrayal, first period, first training bra (it didn't fit), first bra, first apartment, first caviar, first attempt at a Farrah Fawcett hairdo (it didn't work), first new car (I smashed into a guardrail on the highway the first time I took it out), first real job, followed swiftly by the first boss who was certifiably insane.

And I remember the firsts that came after I'd passed out of the treacherous terrain of my teens and twenties: the blessed relief of growing up and realizing that nobody's judgment could define me; that the popular girls' scorn wouldn't kill me; that if the guy I'd nursed a secret crush on didn't like me back, well, that would probably turn out better for both of us in the long run.

If our firsts define us—if how we handle our first sip of stolen beer, our first funeral, our first kiss help turn us into the grownups we become—think of this book as a collection of other women's recipes and road maps, the ingredients and journeys that got them to adulthood.

Or think of it as glimpses of girls and women through imperfectly fastened dressing-room curtains, strangers of eight and thirteen and seventeen and twenty-five posing in front of the mirrors, turning up a collar or rolling down a cuff, considering their faces.

Think of them tossing their hair, batting their lashes, and blowing kisses before leaving the store, mounting their bikes, and riding off into the twilight, toward the future selves who await them.

Virgin

TERRITORY

First Things First:
Introduction

According to Simone de Beauvoir, one is not born a woman, one becomes one. But even though I was born during the heady days of the women's power movement, my own initiation into womanhood was never an issue I greatly considered. Although in retrospect I realized that my six-foot-tall mother was both progressive and spirited (when asked to submit a recipe to the PTA cookbook, she sent me to school with instructions for making a Fluffernutter sandwich), I grew up surrounded by the glorification of male rites of passage, beginning with the fanfare that was my brother David's bar mitzvah. "You're about to become a man" became the oft-repeated mantra in David's thirteenth year. While David shopped for a three-piece suit with a mandatory inside vest pocket (to him, the supreme emblem of manliness), and my parents made a big show of letting him have his first coed nighttime (nighttime!) swim party, the nearly two-years-older sister celebrated her womanhood with a hand-me-down Teenform that once graced the double A's of Sally, a horse-loving girl who lived down the street.

Believe me, I knew that a gently worn bra would not transform me into a woman. Mainly, it just saved me from ridicule when I realized I was the only girl in gym class still wearing an undershirt. The bra failed to impress my parents, always my first audience. "What's the point?" wondered my mother, studying my neatly contained boobs. "You certainly don't need the support." And I clearly remember my father's nonplussed reaction when I greeted him at the door wearing nothing but my boulder holder and a pair of jeans. Not yet modest in front of each other, it would be years before I stopped cuddling under the covers with him or walking in on him while he was shaving, naked, his right leg casually propped up on the sink.

It's true; my family was not the most traditional unit on the block, and casual nudity—my mother once emerged from the bathroom dripping wet and wearing nothing but a brand-new pair of cowboy boots ("They were a little tight so I took a bath with them on so they'd stretch.")—was nothing compared to some of their other stunts. My father, an optometrist, rigged our backyard with stereo speakers in order to play his record album of crow calls, which quickly attracted a Hitchcockian mob of black birds from all corners of the neighborhood.

So what did it? When did my inner de Beauvoir let me know I was finally joining the ranks of womanhood? The bra was a signpost, like the first spin of a bottle, tender bruise of a period cramp, or sneak of a Virginia Slim menthol—big and flashing and necessary and remembered markers along the way, each no more or less important than the rest. But like all good road trips, one event in my journey from girlhood stands out as being so profound, so thrilling, and so upsetting, it can only be described as monumental.

Mine went like this: It was summer; I was almost fifteen, still flat as a board, but tall and willowy, blond and freckled. I realize now that I was pretty back then, but at the time I constantly compared myself to my mother, whose ink-black hair and matching eyes seemed more exotic and glamorous. She moved through life in high heels, made Revlon's Love That Red lipstick her trademark, and enjoyed her reputation among the other town mothers as fashion's final say. My mother was so irresistible to me that when we walked down the street together, I always found myself holding her hand, even if I was sullen and moody, as I often was at fifteen.

When it was hot, my mother didn't like me to hold her hand. She said it made her feel like she couldn't breathe. And the temperature was pushing ninety degrees the day we went walking in downtown Hartford, so I didn't bother to reach for her. We had spent the morning shopping at a local department store, looking for new school boots for me and, after finding a pair, rewarding ourselves with a couple of Brown Cows in the store's eighth-floor Soda Shoppe.

As we crossed Main Street, a humongous truck that had been idling at the stoplight let out an extended blast of the horn. "Hey!" yelled the driver. "Sexy stuff! You're hot!" My mother, who actually loved getting catcalled, turned around and waved in the direction of the truck. "Thanks!" she called cheerily.

"Lady," shouted the trucker, "I was talking to your daughter."

I don't remember what we talked about on the drive home, or whether I felt embarrassed by the driver's attention or responsible for my mother's dismissal. ("Now when someone whistles, I won't know if they're whistling at me or Cathy," she later complained to my father.) But I recognized the significance of being noticed, and the instant attraction to and quick repulsion at being appraised. Why did he pick me instead of my mother, who really didn't look like a mother? (We're sisters, she used to joke when making introductions.) What was he looking at as our long legs marched past his windshield, our strides and gaits so perfectly matched? What if it happened again? And what if it didn't?

It is sad to say that I became a woman the day I was objectified by a man. It's sad because I would be lying if I didn't say I liked it. I was jubilant, actually. I looked at myself in the mirror and finally saw something that was pleasing. Something that could take me places, could get me things. Something that could, and would, get me into all sorts of trouble.

I felt like a woman that day, and it was probably the wrong way to feel in the bra-burning, *Ms.* magazine–reading, equal-rights-marching culture I matured in. And my mother, who through example always provided me with a sense of the strong woman I would eventually become, felt less of one. To be seen as a woman by many in our culture, I learned that day, is to be seen as desirable. But being a woman also means rejecting being pegged as one, as I also saw. It was a conflict that defined my mother back then and that began to define me that sticky, sickly-thrilling day.

These baby steps to womanhood are the inspiration for this book. I began collecting women's coming-of-age stories mostly because they made me feel better about myself. Whenever I would beg my mother, my babysitter, my best friend for a "the first time you" anecdote, it was also an attempt to connect and to understand. Listening to their stories, I would unfailingly feel a me-too-ness with the storyteller. The more intimate the admission, the more resonant my reaction.

I didn't realize the importance of the spoken-word collection until I started repeating them to various audiences: girls'-night-out dinners, cocktail party chatter, bored coworkers. It amazed me how these "first" stories—which always managed to veer away from "After School Special" schmaltz toward self-deprecation—succeeded in uniting a bunch of very different women. Because good stories—really good stories—elicit their own kind of interaction. Even if a story isn't a particularly happy one, the ability to relate, to share, to commiserate is energizing. And a great story, one that is yours but could suitably be anyone's or everyone's, has the capacity to turn a roomful of women into a 1940s musical, a Garland-on-the-clanging-trolley occasion where virtual strangers magically know all the same song and dance steps.

This book really is a first of the firsts: an open-call collection of destinies and denouements, prides and prejudices, virgins and whores. Besides documenting the baby steps from girlhood to womanhood (where the small-scale becomes the large-scale), *Virgin Territory* will pride itself on, to borrow a phrase from Susan Sontag, the "sheer interestingness of the subject."

Survey, select, arrange, appraise, arrange some more. To find the best stories for *Virgin Territory*, I read other women's online diaries and cherry-picked the best (then begged for an interview); sent out massive e-mails in a Fabergé shampoo montage of "and she told a friend, and then she told a friend, and so on, and so on"; and basically talked to any woman who sat down next to me on an airplane, in a cab, on a bar stool: "Hello. Do you remember the first time you saw a naked man?" And then I'd ask them if they had a sister or a mother or a crazy friend I could phone up. Amazingly, they did. Even more amazingly, most allowed me to use their real names. I let those who preferred anonymity to make up their own "stage" names. And occasionally, I altered the names of some of the minor story players—to protect the innocent as well as the guilty.

For me, the variety of voices and the profundity of stories here achieve amazing sweep and power. By interviewing women at various stages in their lives, this book (which is organized to roughly follow the chronological order of experiences in a woman's life) examines how women truly come of age in the age in which they were born. Their stories, while subtle in places, still manage to illuminate the social conventions and consciousness of the times. And while growing up in the 1920s, in the 1950s, in the 1970s, came with its own worries, growing up today still carries many of those same burdens.

Into the Woods

PART I

My first glimpse of things to come materialized from Barbra Streisand. I was spending the night at my grandparents' house, and the three of us sat glued to the television, watching *On a Clear Day You Can See Forever*. In this Technicolor marvel, Streisand's character discovers (and plays out in an assortment of costumes-through-the-centuries) multiple past lives while under hypnosis. In one of her lives, Victorian Barbra wears an anachronistically low-cut gown, and I remember my grandmother leaning over to my grandfather and whispering, "She has the most wonderful cleavage."

Her remark broke my movie spell. I had a pretty impressive vocabulary for an eight-year-old, but I had never encountered this particular word before. "What's cleavage, Grandma?"

"It's the line created when the breasts are pushed together," she explained while my grandfather smoothed an invisible wrinkle in his slacks. "Streisand's cleavage has to be at least six inches."

That did it. Before I wanted boobs or a bra, I wanted cleavage. And better yet, cleavage like Streisand's. A few years later, while watching *Hello, Dolly!*, the words of my grandmother replayed in my mind as Streisand descended the stairs at the Harmonia Gardens. "Just look at that cleavage," I instructed my mother. I spent a lot of time in front of the mirror, my hands a vise, forcing my nonexistent breasts together.

FIRST FROG: KISSING, WARTS AND ALL

p. 46

Becoming a woman happens in a continuum. It has to happen that way because the concept of "woman" is so huge to a flat-chested girl that it can only be achieved a little bit at a time. And the easiest way to understand what it means to become a woman is to define the physical characteristics of

FIRST FRILL: BRAS, DESIGNER JEANS, AND STILETTOS—THE GLITTER BADGES OF WOMANHOOD

p. 71

womanhood—and then to yearn for them, the way I so desperately yearned for cleavage.

The process is so truly random that the only way of getting a grip on the intangible is to focus on the tangible, the visible signs of femaleness: breasts, pubic hair, cheekbones. Why do little girls typically overdo it when playing with their mothers' makeup? It's the meretricious way in which they conjure a woman, in all her purple-eye-shadowed glory.

The process is similar to the tourist who brings home souvenirs from her grand tour of Europe. Ireland gets reduced to a shamrock-embroidered handkerchief; Italy a miniature Colosseum paperweight; France an Eiffel Tower kitchen thermometer. So a girl's simple understanding and slow realization of what it means to be a woman is a transition that's made in sometimes hesitant, sometimes greedy looks through the keyhole to see what's waiting on the other side.

This section of the book reads like a song of myself. It's practically solipsistic, in fact. From stories about bras to tales of the speculum—this part of the journey is strictly body-related, self-related. Every force encountered—a tampon, a razor, a kiss—acts on the storyteller in a purely corporeal way, where often the earliest, most profound truths are embedded.

First Flowering:
Blood, Breasts,
and (Pap) Smears

CHAPTER 1

Thanks, I Needed That

ABBY, MEDICAID ADMINISTRATOR, 31

My entire family was obsessed with my period. For years, every time I saw my grandmother she'd say, "Did you get your monthly yet?" And my mother had already given me a lecture about the evils of tampons. She wasn't very modern about it. She thought they were dirty and unclean, and they were definitely out of the question at my house. She actually wanted to get me the belt, since that's what she and my older sister used. But there was no way I was going to strap one of those things on.

So I took matters into my own hands and sent away for a kit from Stayfree. I think we learned about it in health class. The kit had it all—pads, an informational book about your period. It was great. And I was ready.

I was thirteen and one of the last of my friends to get my period. I was so self-conscious about it. When am I going to get it, when am I going to get it? My friends have it, when I am going to have it? My chest had developed, but where was the rest of it? Come on, I even had the kit!

And of course I had to read the Judy Blume book with Margaret always waiting for her bust and her period.

I was on Kick Line, my high school's version of the Rockettes, and one of the girls bled right through her shorts and I felt bad for her, but I also felt a little jealous. Like she was the mature one and I was still a baby. And I used to listen to stories about cramps and how this one girl's mother used to give her wine for her cramps and I thought that was really adult.

So finally I was in gym class, in uniform and out on the hockey field. My stomach was hurting, but I had no idea what was going on. I always had stomachaches in school and I figured this was just a typical thing. But when I came in off the field and went into the bathroom to change out of uniform—lo and behold!—there it was.

I was so excited. I remember being in between classes, running around looking for my friends, and going, "I got it! I got it!"

That night, as soon as my mother got home from work, I said, "Mom, I got my period." And out of the blue she slapped me. Whack—right across my cheek. I'll never forget it. Then she said, "Welcome to womanhood."

A Little Help from My Friends

SUSAN, BOUTIQUE OWNER, 62

I didn't know how to use a tampon until I got to Cornell. According to Grandma, you couldn't be a virgin and use one. She also told me that you don't French kiss until you get engaged. You know, she was engaged for four years and was a virgin until her wedding night. Hey, this was the old days!

But I hated pads and I hated the belt. That's why you could never go swimming if you had your period, you know. The pad would get soggy in the water, and there was no hiding it. So I got to college and started seeing what was in the bathrooms and what was on my friends' shelves, and I starting asking questions like, "What are those and how do I use them?"

So three of my friends greased up a tampon with Vaseline and shouted instructions from outside my bathroom stall. I think I had to put a mirror between my knees to see what was going on. And I'm taking a while and they're all shouting encouragements like "Come on, Susan! You can do it." And I finally get the thing up there, and I'm thinking, 'This isn't so comfortable.'

So I walk around with it for a while, but it's really hurting me, so I say to one of my friends, "I thought tampons were supposed to be more comfortable than pads."

"They are more comfortable," she says.

"But this thing is killing me," I say.

"Well, did you remember to take the cardboard out?"

When I had been using tampons for a while, I said to Grandma, "It's so much easier. Why would you ever want to walk around feeling like you're wearing a diaper?"

She had never, ever used a tampon. And as far as I know, she had never heard of oral sex either.

Riding the White Horse

STACY, ACTRESS, 37

It's 1976, my grandmother is sixty-three and I am thirteen. The deal was, every summer my mother would send me to Pittsburgh, and I'd spend some time at Lambie's house (that's my grandmother) and some time at my aunt Jeannie's house with my cousin Derek. All summer Derek and I would shuffle back and forth between the two, spending a few weeks here, a few weeks there.

My family was very small. My mom used to say that we had all our family reunions on our couch. So Derek and I were close—because he was an only child too, and we'd been spending our summers together forever. We had all these inside-type jokes. Like, if Derek was acting up, being stupid, I'd say, "That time again?" And he'd say, "No. Just before." There was some Midol commercial on where they'd say that—you know, meaning that there was some PMS going on. So the fact that Derek and I could joke about PMS, well, that shows how close we were.

One day I go into Lambie's bathroom and I see that I started my period. And now I gotta tell my grandma. So I'm like, "Lambie, I started my period."

Her first words are "Derek, go outside."

Now mind you, Derek was all the way down the stairs, far side of the house, in the corner. I mean, he wasn't even on the same floor as us! It was like she was evacuating the house. Like all of a sudden we were some battle station.

And her making Derek go outside—she was immediately setting up the divide between men and women. Like it was wrong for Derek to know that I had my period. And he was my best friend, so I should have been sharing this all with him.

So once he's clear outside, Lambie looks at me and says,

"When did this start?" And I'm so dumbfounded she's asked me this. It's like when you wake up and the phone is ringing. You don't know how long it's been ringing. Is it the first ring, the second?

So I say, "I don't know when it started. It started."

"Well, do you have anything there?"

What she means is, do I have any paraphernalia.

So I tell her, "I got some toilet paper down there."

Now, that means that Lambie has to go walk to the store. And quick.

Now I know the corner store in Homewood, Pennsylvania, couldn't have had what Lambie brought home. I mean, in this small town, you had the guy in town who sold "frush" fish. That's what the sign in his window said. And another guy had turned his basement into a beauty parlor. People were selling penny candy. Batteries. So Lambie had to have gotten on a bus, because Homewood had no kind of drugstore.

Meanwhile, the whole time she's gone, I am sitting there with my legs crossed so tightly, pressed together so closely, I could have put my shoes on backward. Not to mention, if I feel the slightest little thing, I'm back in the bathroom.

So, three toilet paper rolls later . . . Lambie comes home with the equivalent of one of those big brown grocery bags. Because why? She's sixty-three. She has to buy what she knows. She don't know from adhesive strips. She don't know from wings. And she pulls out this box. But the box has only like three pads in it—because they're so big. She takes one out. It's the size of a hero. This submarine sandwich, with all the extra material coming off at the sides at either end of it.

Then she whips out the second box. And it has a belt in it.

Now, there have been several times in my life when my chain-smoking grandma has beaten her own chain-smoking record, and this was one of those times. Here she is staring at me, and I'm staring at her because I don't know what to do with these things, and out comes the pack of cigarettes. And she's trying to figure out the belt without actually getting into it herself and she's chain-smoking, turning the thing around, trying to remember how it goes. And she's explaining to me how to put it on with this cigarette hanging out of her mouth, going, "Here. You do like this." And I'm watching her, hoping she'll draw a diagram or something. Because when I go into the bathroom to actually put the thing on, I just can't get it to work. When I was thirteen, the widest thing about me was my knees. So I'm adjusting and she's chain-smoking, calling out, "What you doing in there?"

My normal panties are now fitting like bikinis, because I got this submarine sandwich down there, it's dragging down my briefs. And my shorts are too tight and I can't walk. You know that song that goes, "If you want to ride, ride the white horse." After this experience, I thought that song was about wearing pads.

I know that I have to hide it all from Derek, because if Lambie sent Derek outside, it must mean that he shouldn't know about it.

And I know that Lambie is helping me all she can—we don't talk about this stuff in my family—and she's in over her head. So she gets on the phone and calls Aunt Jeannie. Derek and I aren't scheduled to go back to Jeannie's, but we go back that night. Lambie figures Jeannie is younger and that it will be easier for me to talk to her.

It must have been my third trip to the bathroom in two hours when Derek finally walks by and knocks on the door.

"Jeez," he says. "What are you doing in there? Dying?"

And I say, "Maybe so."

"Ooh, is it that time again?"

"Yeah," I tell him, "right now."

So that's how Derek found out. And sure enough, Aunt Jeannie says, "Derek, go downstairs!"

Miracle on 34th Street

SHELLEY, LEGISLATIVE REPRESENTATIVE, 32

My parents had been divorced forever, and I had been living with my dad for a while, but this particular area of life I was dreading. All that stuff I'd have to go through—the period, the bra, the sex talk—I wasn't so sure how to go through it all with my father. He was this single guy raising a girl. So in preparation for all that, I moved back home with my mother. I think I was around fourteen maybe. But things didn't go too well with my mother, so I moved back in with my dad.

And it happened two months after that.

I was the second to last of my friends to get my period. So for about a year, you're waiting and waiting for it to come. I remember being most afraid of going swimming, thinking I'd get it in the pool and somehow I'd turn it into the Red Sea or something. And just because my other friends had theirs didn't mean they knew what they were talking about, so I don't remember ever asking them any questions like, "If you get your period in the pool, will it turn the water red?"

One night I'm at my friend Tiffany's house. Tiffany hasn't gotten hers yet either, so we're both just waiting and waiting. Spending all our time waiting for this *thing.* And I go off into the bathroom and *boom.* There it is. And I'm shocked. And when I tell Tiffany about it, her first thought is, "Oh my God, now I'm the last one," not that I've just had some significant moment or anything.

We have to tell Tiffany's mom, who sets me up with some pads. Then I proceed to make phone calls. The first person I call is my mother, who says, "Mazel tov." Then I called all my friends.

It takes me a while to tell my dad. I don't know, but for some reason my friends and I were totally scared to tell our fathers when we finally got our periods. It was as if we had done something wrong. Like you are all of a sudden painfully aware that your father is a guy.

Four days after I first got my period, my dad and I were walking down Third Avenue. I remember we were between 34th and 35th Streets, and I casually said, "Oh, by the way, Dad, I got my period." And my dad just stopped dead in his tracks and said, "Welcome to the real world." Then he gave me a big kiss and we continued walking, never saying another word on the subject.

Beginning the Sentence

MARGARET, WEBMASTER, 27

I was pretty excited about getting my period. It seemed like a really positive thing to have, but I'm not sure why I felt that way, because it wasn't like my friends were all raving about theirs. And when I look back on things, I mostly remember this one girl named Denise who used to be doubled over in the hallways of my middle school, making a big display about her cramps and the fact that she had her period. She'd yell stuff like, "Oh, I'm in pain!" Or she'd be holding on to the wall for support going, "Oh, it hurts so much." She's now an aerobics instructor in Connecticut.

I was fully aware that I hadn't gotten my period yet, and I used to think, "Margaret, you need to get on the ball." So when I finally got my period, in maybe seventh or eighth grade, I was so happy. I guess I saw my period as some new adventure to go on.

It's funny, actually, because now that I think about it, getting my period made me very conscious of the kinds of relationships my girlfriends had with their mothers. I used to see them paired off together and think, "That's really nice." I never felt close to my mom, but at the time, maybe for a small moment, I still had the hope that we could be close in a way that's not possible today.

So after I had my period for about six months, I decided to tell my mother about it, hoping that that would somehow turn us into mother and daughter. But when I came to her, she said something like, "Well, now you know what you have to look forward to for the next thirty years." Her reaction, which was so opposite from my initial feelings, made me realize that we were always going to be at odds. I saw my period as liberating; my mother saw it as some kind of sentence.

Whatever, Mom

NICOLE, SEVENTH GRADER, 13

I got my period for the first time last week. I just woke up and it was there. I wasn't excited at all. And I don't like it. It's gross.

The day I got it, which was Friday, I didn't have school. I felt like I had a stomachache, so I went to the bathroom. I knew what it was. I told my mom, and she just said, "Well, go get a pad."

It wasn't like when my friend Lindsay got hers. She got it in school, in her chair, and she didn't even know it. So after class she got up, and the chair was dirty and some of the kids were teasing her. They were saying stuff like, "I'm not touching that desk!"

I'm not really embarrassed about it. My mom got me *What's Happening to My Body? Book for Girls* for Christmas and told me to read it, and if I had any questions, I could ask her. But I didn't have any. I already learned about periods when I was in fifth grade.

I don't know if my mom told my dad about it. I kinda think my brother knows. He probably thinks it's really nasty.

Pack It in

MARY, EXECUTIVE RECRUITER, 34

An hour before my eighth-grade championship basketball game, my "friend" paid me a visit for the first time. I was panic-stricken and in tears, and since no one was home that particular hour, I was left to my own devices. Calling in sick was considered but quickly ruled out because, as a star player, it meant risking the championship. So I wadded-up a roll of toilet paper as big as my skull—I needed to be well protected for the big game—and attached it to my underwear with electrical tape.

Moments later a car honked. It was my friend's mom, Mrs. Solger, who was picking me up for the big game. Since I had a skull between my legs, I was walking a bit funny. Mrs. Solger asked me about my new swagger, and I told her my muscles were still sore from last week's game.

Unfortunately, the electrical tape was not a foolproof plan. During the game the wad started shifting in my shorts. First it shifted up to the center of my buttocks. I was mortified 'cause it looked like I had taken a big dump. I quickly shoved it back into position. Then, when I was at the free throw line, I noticed that it had shifted to my left side. The other players were staring at it in amazement. Some probably theorized that it was some type of tumor, which explains the sympathetic looks.

I shoved it back into position. Then, to make matters worse, the toilet paper started unraveling as I was running up and down the court. People in the stands were laughing and pointing at me, as this long strand of bloody white Charmin was trailing behind me.

I had to call a time-out during a crucial moment in the game, to my coaches' horror, so that I could reapply some new tape.

I thought I would never forget this mortifying display of athleticism. But actually, today I can't even remember if we won or lost the big game.

A Bumpy Road
KAE, PUBLISHER, 58

My mother was very concerned that I know all about periods and that I never have a frightening experience. When she was a young girl, back in the 1920s, her mother did tell her that she would be having a period and explained how to handle it. But she lived in a small town in Nebraska, and a lot of the girls didn't know, and one day my mother found one of her best friends standing in a farm pond crying. She told my mother that she was dying and that she didn't know what to do. And my mom helped her out of the pond, and her little friend said, "I'm bleeding to death, I'm dying, I must have some awful disease." So my mom had to explain to her about periods. And so she really worried about those girls who weren't told about periods, because it could be such a traumatic experience if suddenly you're bleeding and you have no idea why. And she really was very concerned about that.

I was born in Denver in 1944—so I would imagine this was about 1954. My mother sent away to the big sanitary napkin manufacturer—in those days it was Kotex—for a kit. We didn't have tampons, or at least my mother didn't think they were for nice girls. And so she sent away, and they had this book that they would provide to you, plus free samples, and a sanitary napkin belt, because back then they didn't have the stick-on pads. You had to wear this hideous belt. And so she sent for this whole kit that apparently the company had created for mothers to sit down with and talk to their daughters.

She sat down and told me all about periods and told me to read the book. I still remember the line that read, "Only big girls and women menstruate." And I thought, "Oh my God, I cannot wait!" I was so excited; I kept that kit in a special place in my room and read the book over and over. Soon I was a menstruation expert.

But somehow we didn't get into breasts. Either it slipped her mind, or she had never thought about it. But she should have, because at about that time or shortly thereafter our very close friend who lived across the street—she was a woman with no children of her own, but my mother's best friend and she was really good to me, and she and her husband used to watch me when my mom had to be away . . . lovely people—this woman named Jeri all of a sudden was in the hospital, and I heard my mother talking to her friends about it. Nobody ever really told me much except that Jeri had to have her breasts removed and she had cancer because she had a lump in her breast. Everybody spoke about this in hushed tones.

I got the idea that this was a very grave situation. Jeri had cancer and she might not live. It started with this lump in her breast. And so I was all set up for disaster. About that time, maybe a week or two later, I was taking a bath and I started washing my chest and all of a sudden I felt under my nipple this lump and I thought, "Oh my God, I've got what Jeri had!" And for some reason, I never wanted to give my mother bad news. My mother had polio when she was a young girl, so I was always trying not to upset her. I remember once I skinned my knee. I rolled over on my bike and really hurt my leg, and it got infected, and I wouldn't tell her that I was really in trouble.

And so I suffered by myself for about a week, thinking I was going to die of breast cancer just like Jeri did. Finally, I don't remember exactly how it happened, but I do remember going to my mom and crying and showing her and her going, "Oh my goodness, this is just the beginning of your breasts, this is nothing to worry about!" And I remember she even was laughing—not in a mean way—but I remember feeling really silly. It was a traumatic experience but I got over it quickly, and as my breasts developed it wasn't a trauma anymore, and pretty soon I was just looking forward to getting a bra.

Two for the Team

When did I know I was different? That I was changing? That I was a woman? That I had to be different? That I had to be different because society decided that I needed to be different? I realized that when I had to put on my first bra.

Up until that time I was a tomboy. I was always around boys, was always climbing trees, always having rock fights with them. We would set up metal chairs, and across the alley—because we lived in Baltimore—we used to throw rocks back and forth and see who could get hurt the most. I didn't think I was any different from any boy. I always wanted to be a boy. I thought boys had it made. Boys were less encumbered; they were freer. The world was their oyster. Girls had to be so careful about what we did and how we did it, according to our mothers.

I always had a very "survival of the fittest" attitude that, growing up female in the 1950s, was not the way to survive. Women were supposed to share, they were supposed to be compassionate, be giving. And I wasn't. I never played with dolls. I had one doll, and I remember burying it in a Florsheim shoebox under my parents' window, swearing at the age of twelve that I would never get married and never have children. I didn't want to be like the kind of females who were supposedly my role models—like my mother, my aunts, all the housewives who basically stayed home while the men went to work, and who seemed very unhappy and very frustrated. You know, who kvetched over the back fence, had coffee klatches. That wasn't what I wanted, but at that point no one had told me that I could do or become anything I wanted. My grandmother wanted me to be a nurse, my father wanted me to get married, and I wanted to be an archaeologist.

And then I started growing up. I started maturing, in ways that

were very very odd. I started having a lot of pain in
I didn't really know what that pain was. And my
wasn't the kind of mother who was going to sit down and t.
those things. And so I just kept fighting, I kept wrestling, I kept
playing football.

I was thirteen. I had very short hair and always wore a baseball
cap; I tried to look like a boy. This concerned my mother, who told
me, "You know, you've got to start acting like a little lady." And I
didn't know what that meant. I saw all my little friends with their
cute little dresses and their dolls, and I knew that was not what I
wanted to be. So I didn't listen to her.

One day the neighborhood guys and I were playing football,
and this guy who was a whole lot shorter than me ran full blast
into my very sore chest. And as I went home with my arms criss-
crossed over my chest, I realized that I had to start wearing a bra.
And to this day I hate bras; it's the first thing that comes off when
I walk in the door. And I still don't wear them on weekends.

Nothing Comes Free

AMY, COLLEGE SENIOR, 21

I've been with the same guy for two years, so it's not like my
mom doesn't know what we're doing. She's a nurse and has
worked in so many different fields, including gynecology, so she
was more concerned that I hadn't been to a gynecologist yet and
I was twenty years old. So she was like, "Are you interested in
birth control?" And I was like, "Yeah, whatever." Half my friends
haven't even told their parents that they're having sex, and they're
all twenty-one or older. And I'm like, "Whatever, man!" My mom
is so cool about stuff like that.

My mom offered to make an appointment for me, which was

fine, but I told her, "I do not want some man or woman that you know examining me. I don't want the whole appointment to be about you."

It's already an embarrassing thing. Especially your first time. So I didn't exactly want to be sitting in the office and have some woman walk in and be like, "Oh my God, I know your mom!" That's like having sex and having the family picture right next to you. It's too weird for me.

But my mom goes ahead and makes an appointment with a woman she went to nursing school with, a nurse practitioner. So this lady definitely knows my mother. And she thinks we're like blood related, since she knows my mother, so she says, "I have a favor to ask of you." Because, of course, we're so close at this point.

And she's like, "Oh, I have this student, do you mind if she helps with the exam?" I'm too shocked to say anything. I guess I mutter, "Yeah, whatever," or something that sounds like that. And in walks this peppy blond hey-I-love-doing-this kind of woman. And it is not fitting my mood at all.

They tag team. They do it all at once. They are both at the same end of the table, joking about how I'm being double-teamed. It feels like a threesome, seriously.

They are fighting over who is going to give me STD tests, and I'm like, "Oh my God! You have to be kidding me." How embarrassing is that? It takes me twenty minutes to even ask for those tests, and now they're fighting over which one they're going to give me. The student is like, "I call herpes!"

Then they're fighting over the breast exam. My nurse practitioner starts on the right side, and then she's like, "Hey, whatever your name is, why don't you come up here and do the left one?" They both totally feel me up.

They just joke the whole time, almost like they're bickering, but not really.

At one point my nurse practitioner can't find the lube and is like, "I hate it when I lose my K-Y jelly!" And the other woman is like, "Yeah, but it feels so good!" And I'm like, "Oh my God! Are you kidding me?" 'Cause I don't use K-Y otherwise. I don't know about things like that or what they're supposed to do.

I wasn't offended. I don't offend easily at all. But it was hysterical because it was happening to me. I knew that my cell phone was in my car and as soon as I got to my car, I was going to call everybody I knew and tell them my story.

At least I got my birth control pills. For free! Thank you!

Unholy Virgin

ANDREA, MARKETING MANAGER, 28

I was fifteen years old, and my mom decided it was time for me to go to the gynecologist for my first checkup. I was nervous going in because I was very sexually inexperienced. Even though I had gotten my period when I was eleven, I had never even used a tampon, so I was really unfamiliar with anything going on down there. I think maybe I knew a little of what was involved as far as being examined, but I didn't know about the stirrups or the speculum, and I don't remember if I asked my mother anything about what was going to happen, but I doubt I did.

The doctor seemed to me like he was about eighty. Maybe he wasn't really that old, but he was definitely grandfatherly. He was my mom's gynecologist, but she didn't come into the room with me. She just drove me and stayed out in the waiting room.

I know I was really nervous, and when the doctor began to examine me, I must have started to tense up. Then I started crying, because it was hurting. There was a nurse who came in the room to try and distract me and talk to me. I don't remember what she was talking to me about—probably small talk about high school.

41

I was squirming, instinctively trying to wriggle away from the doctor, so she was also holding me down, talking to me and holding me down so the doctor could examine me. And I was crying during all of this.

I guess the doctor thought it would help matters if there were even more to distract me. So he grabbed the hand mirror, sat me up a little, and had me, *me* hold the hand mirror down to myself so I could watch what he was doing. And as he's busy going through his examination, he's pointing out the parts and naming the parts. That was unbearable. I may have looked a little bit, but the whole thing of trying to hold the mirror and sit there—it was definitely keeping me busy but it just was not a good thing. I just wanted him to be done as soon as possible.

He finally finished, and jokingly he said to me, and I knew at the time he was kidding, "No man is ever going to fit down there," because I was so small down there. And I kind of laughed, ha ha, whatever. I told my mom I was never going back to any doctor, let alone that doctor. I'd had it. And she felt horrible, really bad. She may have even taken me out to lunch afterward because she was feeling so guilty.

I told my boyfriend at the time about the visit, I'm sure without going into any detail. I probably said it was pretty painful and everything. I said to him what the doctor told me about how no man was ever going to be able to fit down there, and I was kind of laughing as I said it. We were both in our sophomore year in high school, I don't think either one of us had our driver's license yet, so he certainly wouldn't have known if I had a hole or not.

And *this* is the part I found out about later. He told his best friend what the doctor had told me, thinking that the doctor was serious, and the best friend told someone and then someone told someone and someone told someone.

There were actually two different versions of the rumor, I found out later. One was that I had no hole and that my parents said they were going to wait until I was eighteen to have the operation to make a hole. The other version was that I had a hole, but it was covered up by skin. Again, the part about being eighteen and getting the hole at eighteen, that part was in both versions, that my parents were going to be keeping me from having sex until I was legal.

I found out about the rumor, which had gone completely around the school, about a year later. I was at a party, and a friend of mine who was really girly—captain of the cheerleading squad and really really super blunt—came up to me and asked me how I was able to get my period. And I was like, "What?" I mean, we probably had been drinking a little, but I really didn't understand why she was asking me this. And that's when she said, "Well, I heard you had some problems and had this hole that was covered up. What's going on, and when are you having the operation?"

At first I just started laughing, because she was so funny, so I thought what she was asking was funny, too. When I asked her more about it, some more people chimed in and said that they had heard about my hole, too. And some of my friends had known about the rumor for a while, but they didn't want to tell me about it, since they knew it wasn't true.

I was never mad. And I was never really angry with my boyfriend, although I think I finally confronted him with it. But these boys were all around sixteen or seventeen, and it wasn't like they were being malicious. I know they were genuinely concerned. I could see how, after I told my boyfriend about what the doctor said, these guys could think it was serious. But I never remember feeling that people were making fun of me or laughing at me.

I went to high school in Dumfries, Virginia, and everyone there was just so open with each other. I really didn't think it was weird that my sexuality was something that was discussed among people. I went to my ten-year reunion, and I'm sure that there were people there who still think I'm missing something.

Giddy Up
GRACE, PRESS SECRETARY, 28

I started my period when I was sixteen and living in Italy. My dad was in the navy, and we were stationed there. My periods were lasting ten or twelve days and my mother was concerned, so she made me an appointment with the military doctor. I had never had an "exam" like this before, and my mother said, "Honey, I know you're nervous, but it will be all right." Then she gave me a Valium.

My best friend Becca drove me to the appointment. The doctor drew out a diagram and started pointing to pictures, explaining what she was going to be doing. I was totally freaking out. The more I heard about it, the more anxious I got, because my imagination was way worse than the reality of the situation. I was especially afraid about spreading my legs.

The doctor leads me into this room, and there's a nurse in there who shows me the examining table. All the while she's calling out instructions: "Put your head at that end, lay down, feet go there . . ." Then she leaves.

I completely panic because I haven't paid attention to what she was telling me. All I know is that I'm supposed to get undressed and get on the table. I'm pretty out of it because of the Valium, and on top of that I'm not exactly sure what the stirrups are. I've never seen anything like them before.

Against my better judgment, I lay down on the table the wrong way, with my elbows back in the stirrups. I'm tilted downward, with my feet elevated higher than my head. The doctor taps on the door and comes back in with the nurse, and they both start howling. The doctor says, "No, honey. It's not your elbows that go there."

I'm so humiliated. I ask, "Has anyone ever made this mistake before?" After I turn myself around, they stop laughing at me—in front of me anyway.

First Frog: Kissing, Warts and All

CHAPTER 2

Sloppy Seconds

LUNA, ONLINE TRAVEL AGENT, 23

When I was in grade school, I was painfully shy. I had a mouthful of retainers and thick glasses. I had only one real friend. Her name was Amber.

Because I was so shy, I was usually the object of pranks and dares. It had become known in the class that I had a crush on the cutest boy in class, Brandon. He was a grade-school Adonis, with blond hair and blue eyes and a whole lot of confidence.

One day several of Brandon's friends circled me and started taunting me, "Luna likes Brandon, Luna likes Brandon." I wanted to run away and hide desperately, but there was nowhere to go.

Finally Brandon's best friend, David, stepped out of the circle and told me they had a dare for me.

They dared me to French-kiss Brandon in front of everyone under the old tree in the corner of the playground after lunch the next day.

To say the least, I was mortified. I had never kissed anyone before! Let alone French-kissed, and I didn't know how, and it wasn't exactly something I could go home and ask my mom about.

So I asked my friend Amber.

The next day at lunch Amber and I went to the girls' bathroom. After checking to be sure there was no one in any of the stalls, we entered the large wheelchair-accessible stall on the far end of the restroom together.

I removed my retainers, one off the top, one off the bottom, and stuffed them in my pocket and waited for the lesson to begin.

Amber began by showing me basic kissing techniques on her arm. "Pucker your lips like a fish, then smack . . . mmmmaaa." Then we moved on to the French kissing. "Open your mouth and stick your tongue half way out. Now swirl."

We were bent over laughing so hard, and I'm sure our hysterics must have been heard all the way down the hall, but no one bothered us.

Finally, the bell rang and lunch was over, the time was here and I was petrified. "Amber! I can't do this! I will look like a dork!" I was nearly in tears I was so scared.

"Here, like this . . ." and Amber put her hand behind my neck and pulled me to her. She kissed my lips, and then parted her mouth. It felt very natural. I did the same, and we French kissed.

My heart was racing when I realized what we'd done, and we both stared at each other for a moment before we burst into laughter. We grabbed our books and ran out of the bathroom together, almost knocking over the playground aide on our way out the door.

I met Brandon and the rest of the class, under the big tree in the corner of the playground, and I did kiss Brandon. Amber was right behind me, and I didn't look like a dork at all. I looked like a twelve-year-old having her second kiss.

The Spins
CAREN, ART DIRECTOR, 41

My first kiss experience was kind of, well, yucky. I still had a mouth full of braces, and I remember I was wearing a stupid "smiley face" T-shirt. I was visiting my dad in Lancaster, Pennsylvania. And there were a bunch of kids that I used to hang around with when I visited on the weekends. I must have been twelve.

We were all out one night, and somebody decided we should play Spin the Bottle. I remember being nervous. I was still pretty young, and intensely self-conscious.

The other kids were okay . . . your basic bunch of prepubescent boys (and they all have that funny hormonal smell). Within the first couple of spins, the bottle came to a slow stop, pointed right at me. The next thing I knew, one of the boys jumped on top of me and stuck his tongue in my mouth.

It's amazing I didn't become a lesbian after that. I still can't remember any of their names or faces. I just remember the humid night air, the cool grass, and my complete and total revulsion.

House of the Rising Son
MELISSA, JOURNALIST, 31

When I was twelve, I came back from summer camp with a hugely embellished story of my first kiss. I went to an all-girls summer camp, and any of our rare "socials" with the boys' camps across the lake threw us all into a state of mass hysteria. For weeks all anyone talked about was what she was going to wear. So when Matt from Manhattan asked me to dance, I think I was already primed for the kind of time-altering hormonal surge that only makes sense when it's felt from the inside. Now, I can no longer distinguish the expectations from the reality. Did I feel his bulge press against me when we danced? How many dances did we dance? But I was shy, and I eventually made excuses to get away. At the end of the evening, I saw him searching me out, but I was too distraught to give him any opportunities to actually give me a kiss. But I wanted so badly to have kissed him. And so the memory of those expectations and longings somehow got incorporated into a falsehood that I retold as reality.

My actual first kiss didn't come until two years later, when I was fourteen. I spent the night at my girlfriend Erin's house. She had an older brother, David, who was sixteen. He had freckles and a skinny chest. He went to an all-boys Catholic school, and somehow he didn't strike me as the popular type. But I thought he was funny and charming. He made me laugh, and he was comfortable enough with us girls to wrestle and hang out with us.

We began the evening with another mind-altering first. After spinning around and around and hyperventilating, David would grab one of us tightly from behind—right under our armpits—and squeeze, which of course induced fainting. The blackout only lasted seconds, but to us, the experience lasted much longer. Heady stuff.

Later that night we gave each other backrubs. My girlfriends and I were used to taking turns, or sitting in circles, to give each other backrubs, and I think I felt honored that David found us interesting enough to want to spend his time with us. Eventually Erin fell asleep. With my shirt partially off, David continued to caress me, and I remember wanting that growing thrill to continue.

What was going through my mind at that point? I was in that

state of semifear mixed with teenage hormonal tingling. I remember his fingers running down the sides of my back, from my underarms to my waist. I remember wondering if what was going on was what I thought was going on. He was getting more intimate than what the typical backrub required. I was wondering if he would actually touch my breast. I think I made it easier for him by shifting positions. Eventually his hands found their way to my front, and we began to kiss. But that's about all! I had no concept of or desire for sex. (Much changed in the following two years!) And of course I was concerned that Erin would wake up.

Then the door flew open. Erin's parents stood there, mouths agape, as they witnessed me with my shirt off and our bodies partially intermingled. I didn't hear them come home, didn't hear them climb the steps, nothing. Just lost in that sensual moment that went oh so wrong!

The father just yelled, "David!" He didn't have to say anything else. David scrambled out, his parents followed, and the door shut, leaving me alone with my friend who was still asleep.

I was utterly mortified. I went downstairs and paced the living room for a while. Should I leave? Should I apologize to the parents? Finally I went back to bed and eventually fell asleep.

Afterward the mother was always a bit cold toward me. The father, however, told me years later that I was always their favorite of Erin's friends.

The Foreign Tongue
ELIZABETH, POET, 49

It's hard to forget someone with a name like Boonrak Boonyaketmala.

I was fifteen and was invited to a party hosted by my best

friend Peggy's parents. The party was for the AFS, which stands for American Field Service, a foreign exchange program where teenagers from all over the world would attend high schools in this country. Peggy and I were both part of the AFS club, even though our families weren't host families until a year later. Basically, we just befriended the foreign students who were in our school, made sure they knew their way around, and introduced them to the other kids.

At the end of the school year, all the AFS students, including the ones from my school, got on buses and did a three-week tour of the United States. At the end of June, they came to Vermont. I can't imagine why they would want to come to Vermont in June, but they did. And Peggy's parents agreed to host a costume party for them.

I was at an age where I wanted to look good, and I remember taking great care in choosing my costume. Since I fancied myself as something of a free spirit, I decided to go as a gypsy. I wore a wide skirt that billowed when I twirled in front of the mirror, hoop earrings, and a white peasant blouse. My mother took a picture of me, posing with a rose between my teeth! It's still probably somewhere at her house.

I loved to go barefoot, which was part of my whole free spirit image. (These were the days when I thought I'd never live in the suburbs.) So the minute I got to my friend's house, off came the sandals. I remember that Boonrak was attracted by the fact that I went barefoot. He actually bought my free spirit image.

The clouds of time have covered my memory of where Boonrak went to school that year, but it wasn't anywhere near Vermont. What I do recall is that he was foreign and exciting and it was a moment in time, a one-time adventure.

I don't think the earth moved when he kissed me, but I sure was thrilled. It was my very first kiss! It was just a gentle brushing of the lips, very chaste, but my stomach lurched up and down. We spent the evening snuggling, cuddling, and kissing. I was most excited because he was very handsome, small and slender with cocoa-butter-colored skin and a smooth, hairless face. And he was so sweet.

He was around eighteen, and he was going home to Thailand to get married. He had been engaged since he was five years old, and he hadn't seen this woman since that time. He talked about how nervous he was to go back home and see her again, and wondered what she would be like and if they would have anything in common.

We wrote to each other at least once a month for two years. I still have his letters somewhere. I haven't looked at them for nearly thirty years, but they're there.

I remember later someone telling me that Boonrak had a girl in every city he went to during his three-week tour. If he wrote to them as faithfully as he did to me, he must have been very busy those two years!

When my last letter was not answered, I assumed he had gotten married. I do still think of him from time to time when I go barefoot. I will say that.

Seeing Stars
STEPH, WEBSITE DEVELOPER, 26

I was *sooo* boy crazy in elementary school. I'd write my name plus MW (or CK or JD or whoever) all over my notebook, and then have to get a new notebook every other week.

All the girls used to make lists of what we liked about the boys—we'd give them points for being cute, good at sports, nice, smart, strong. I can't remember what else mattered.

I don't remember my first kiss. I'm not even sure what counts as my first kiss. Maybe it came from my first boyfriend, Mark. During recess we used to play Spin the Bottle and all those other silly kissing games you play when you're in third grade. There was this one time when me and my boyfriend and my friend and her boyfriend were going to kiss in the woods. The whole school found out, and everyone was hiding in the woods to watch. We all got in trouble and had to write a note to the principal about what we were doing. Thankfully everyone said they were there to watch my friend kiss and not me. But no kissing happened that day.

I do remember another boyfriend who was the new boy in school. When we went to kiss in the woods, he put his arms around me and kissed me on the lips. The other couple (yes, we always did this in twos) was shocked. Then all the boys in school made fun of my boyfriend for his "movie kiss," and all the girls were jealous of me.

Size Matters

BETTY, DRUMMER, 36

He smoked. He played hooky. He was the type your mom *and* dad warned you about. He was my brother's friend, two years older than me, and twice as wide. He was really, really fat. Enormous. And I kid you not, his last name was Sizemore. He gave me my first kiss.

I was in the fifth grade, and we had just moved to the country. I rode the bus to school. It was the kind of bus where the kids in the back cranked AC/DC and "Highway to Hell" sounded warped and warbly because the batteries were always about to run out. They played it louder than the little speakers could handle, so it sounded all distorted too, like a muffled principal's announcement coming across the public address system. Kids ran wild, hopping from seat to seat, gossiping, and punching, and pinching.

I was sitting reading *The Hobbit* when Sizemore yelled, *"Hey Betty, get over here!"* So I went over and asked what he wanted. I was scared.

He made me sit on the inside, and he trapped me against the wall of the bus. It was a hot day to begin with, and his huge body pressing into me made me sweat. I couldn't breathe. He told me to give him a kiss. So I did like he said.

His stringy black hair hung down around my face, his fat engulfed my skinny body. But his lips were soft and wet.

I kissed him twice before we pulled up to my house. I raced off the bus, insane, not knowing what I was feeling. I ran into my room and shut the door. Then I looked at myself in the dresser mirror and told myself, "I kissed a boy . . . uh, hey, I have a boyfriend!"

I packed up my stuffed animals, my Barbie dolls, and my glitter stickers, crammed them into a Glad trash bag, and tossed them out on the curb. Only girls play with toys, and I was all grown up.

He never kissed me again, and I was too timid to approach him. In any event I forgot about him in a week, missed my toys, and wished I still had them. I went back to thinking about horses and saving to buy an Easy Bake Oven.

I heard later that he got religion and went around carrying a Bible and preaching to sinners at shopping malls.

Taking the Lead

SARA, DATABASE OPERATIONS MANAGER, 59

This was the boy that I knew I must marry. It was something I knew before the kiss even happened. To me, what predates the kiss is even more extraordinary. So I have to tell that story first.

We must have been fourteen, and he was so cute. His name was Timmy, and he had brown hair, and there was always at least one piece sticking straight up. I didn't know to call it a cowlick back then. He was short, but I was shorter. And he had one of those soft, round faces. He had a big brother, the most popular guy in school. My group of friends and I all talked about his brother (whose name I won't mention) because we knew he "did it" with a girl who was a whole year older. It was information we all found very appealing.

I *knew* that Timmy would grow up to be just like his big brother. But at the time Timmy wasn't a real kingpin at school.

Timmy stood on the riser behind me in eighth-grade chorus class. During one performance, he put one of his hands, pressed it, into my shoulder blade. But he did it in a way so no one could tell he was touching me. Oh, what it felt like! His hand, I'm telling you, was fused to my body—it was so hot. Fused! Oh, the heat that hand was creating between us.

A few days later, maybe that weekend, we went ice-skating along the Delaware River. That's where all the kids went. There was a rock there that we all called Kissing Rock, and I knew that was where Timmy was leading me to. And I allowed him to lead me. There was this huge recognition that I was choosing this path—and that no one was forcing me or pushing me. It was very collaborative—the way I've always liked sex to be, actually.

As we were skating toward Kissing Rock, the buildup was just incredible. I was really "in" it; it wasn't being done to me. It was a completely different delight.

Timmy's lips were surprisingly soft. Melting soft. But what I remember most was the skate over to the kiss. When I think about it now, my decision to go to the Rock was a huge introduction to myself. Does this make sense?

He moved away at the end of ninth grade. So we didn't get married.

First Fixing:
Hair Free and Fat Free—
Bod Is in the Details

CHAPTER 3

I Shave, Therefore I Am

SHEILA, LAWYER, 31

My defining moment would have to be my first razor. I don't know how old I was, but I was still in elementary school, and still at an age when summer camp was part of my life.

I was shopping with my mother for camp supplies—tiny shampoos, tiny soaps, tiny things that she wouldn't mind my losing at camp, because I almost certainly would. There were razors and blades in the spontaneous-purchase section of the checkout lane, and I asked my mom what it was like to shave her legs. The idea of drawing something that sharp up my skinny little legs just terrified me, but I figured I was going to have to do it someday—

nonconformity had not yet occurred to me as an option. She said it didn't hurt at all, as long as you were careful, and then she actually bought me my own, for some day when I might want to use it.

Thinking about it, I'm not sure why she bought me one. She had one, of course, a heavy silver single-bladed thing, and she and I shared a bathroom. She might have wanted the excuse to indulge herself in what then passed for New Razor Technology, or she might have been worried that I really would hurt myself if I tried to use hers.

Anyway, I stared at it for about a week, and suddenly naked-legged girls were everywhere I looked. I felt like such a baby for *not* shaving my legs, and it became intolerable to think of going off to camp as the last female denizen of the earth who wasn't mature enough to shave her legs. So I did, the night before I got on the bus. I cut myself in a couple places, which hurt like hell, but I still felt pretty cool.

I got to camp with my new razor and an extra blade or two, and it turned out that this was not only my first razor, it was the first razor belonging to anyone in my cabin. The girl who went on to become a cheerleader didn't shave her legs yet, and the girl who had already had three boyfriends (and *kissed* one of them, if you can imagine such a thing) had never shaved her legs. I played it cool, of course, as though I'd been shaving since I could pick up a razor. By the time camp was over, two weeks later, we were all shaving. Our legs looked like we'd been attacked by eight-inch-tall psychopaths with teeny little knives—but they were smooth, and by God, we were *women*.

The Beast Within

CORINNA, POLICY ANALYST, 31

This story takes place in Dallas, circa 1979, in the heat, heat, heat of a Texas summer. The bathtub I defiled was in a second-story apartment walk-up that I shared with my mom.

For a while, when I was in third grade and my mom was working on getting her act together, I spent a lot of time over at my cousin's house. She was this little rich girl and had all the things I desperately wanted, like a closet full of beautiful sundresses. There was this one dress, yellow gingham with little tie straps at the shoulders. I wanted so much to be like a girl who would wear this dress.

So I borrowed this sweet yellow dress. I put it on and looked in the mirror and thought I was the cutest thing ever. I borrowed her white sandals too, which were strappy and bare and what I thought were the ultimate in femininity.

I walked into school and wanted to be beautiful and pretty, but all day no one said anything about my dress or my white shoes. When I got outside for recess, I headed to the swings, because I wanted to make this pretty little dress flutter out all girly-like. Maybe it was because I was swinging, and for the first time all day my legs were at eye level, but all of a sudden these two boys were watching me. One of them said, "Do you know you have hairy legs?"

It was true. I had the hairiest legs for an eight-year-old. My father is Greek. And of course it didn't help that my hair was black and my skin was so white.

The boys started calling me Gorilla Girl. I was devastated. The whole rest of the day I had to go around with my hairy legs poking out of that beautiful dress. It was the first day I knew that girls shouldn't have hair down there.

When I got home, I said, "Mom, can I shave?" and she said, "No."

She didn't understand what I was saying. "No, Mom," I said, "I'm *going* to shave."

And I got in the bathtub and pretty soon there was hair everywhere. Just everywhere. Thick, clumps of my gorilla hair—on the sides of the tub, in the drain, on the soap—everywhere.

That was the beginning of me being self-conscious about my legs, my hair, myself. And to this day I have this hidden fear of being exposed as Gorilla Girl—always. Gorilla Girl lives within.

She completely represents how I don't measure up.

Southern Roots
SUSAN, ACTRESS, 36

I'm from Oklahoma. Not the Deep South, but south enough to understand that hair is everything. Big, blond, hot-rollered, Miss America hair. Big, big, big. For years my mother, every six weeks or so, would announce it was "rut" day. At first I wasn't sure what she was talking about, but this being the South, I finally figured out that "ruts" were "roots," as in "We're going to watch that Alex Haley miniseries *Ruts*." Or "Hey, get out in the backyard and pull up those weeds by their ruts."

So when it was rut day, we would hop into her Buick Regal that she'd left outside with the air-conditioning running to cool it down for a half-hour, and we would drive about three blocks (because nobody walks in Oklahoma) over to her friend Caroline's, and Caroline would spend the rest of the day doing Mother's ruts. At first she would just paint on the color, and then occasionally Caroline came out with the plastic skullcap with the holes all in it, and she would take this thing that looked like a crochet needle and shove it in Mother's head and pull that hair out. So she would do only select ruts. These were neighborhood ladies posing as suburban chemists, trying to get just the right look.

I had naturally blond hair, so I didn't quite get it. After going to this woman's house about every six weeks or so, and seeing Mother get her ruts done, it was amazing to see this transformation from before to after. Her entire self-esteem changed.

At around fourteen, I realized I wasn't going to be blond all my life and that probably, at some point, I was going to have a rut day of my own. When I was sixteen, Mother announced that I should get my ruts done. I was afraid to go to Caroline because I thought if I was going to get my ruts done, I should go to a professional salon instead of a suburban housewife. So she took me to the local salon and had some young guy do my ruts. And it was amazing. I thought I had pretty high self-esteem before I went in. But when we were finished, I remember looking in the mirror and saying, "Oh my God." I felt older, I felt like a woman, I felt at sixteen sexier, I felt grown up.

And then I realized, well no wonder Mother gets her ruts done! It's like a high, and you just keep going back and back and back. And it's not against the law! Little did I realize, of course, that once you got your ruts done, you had to keep getting your ruts done. From that moment forward I would have the responsibility of ruts and all that came with it. You're just not allowed to stop. My mother is sixty-something years old, and she's still getting her ruts done. If it ain't broke, don't fix it.

Jheri-Rigged
JANICE, CUSTOMER SUPPORT, 32

I was born in Iowa City, Iowa, and whisked away shortly after birth to Sierra Leone, West Africa, before I could even say the word *corn*. I spent my childhood and teenage years growing up in the capital city called Freetown. But by the time I got to secondary school in Freetown, my parents decided to ship all their children back to the United States.

This was about the time I was coming into my own with friends, with boys, and just trying to be a little popular and less shy. Why shy? As a child, I was always concerned about how the other kids saw me. I had a big belly button, so I never wore two-piece bathing suits at the pool. I was self-conscious of my behind because my skin tone was all shades of brown but a little browner around the cheeks. And the hair—oh my goodness, the hair. What a little African girl wouldn't do to have long, blond, straight Barbie Doll hair!!!! Well, the hair was just a nightmare all its own.

I remember in the good old 1980s (a shameful decade I just want to forget), the hottest thing was not getting your hair straightened with a hot comb but getting it processed and curled up soaking in some crap called Jheri Curl. Ouch! To me, the Jheri Curl was the hottest, hippest thing, not to mention the closest thing to being Westernized!!!! Ever wonder why having your hair dripping with liquid, all curled up and sticky, would be considered hip? I honestly have absolutely no clue. Well, I got my Jheri Curl, and I was ready to leave Africa for the United States to show the Americans, "I'm cool and 'now' and just like you!"

Wow. What a rude-ass awakening I got. Not only had Jheri Curls gone out of style, but they had been replaced by straight perms, bangs, Capezios, Sergio Valente jeans, and those darn tiny-ass Jordache pocketbooks, which came in all these girly, pretty colors. I wondered, "Where are all the Jheri Curl people I saw in the movies back home? Gone! Like the hairstyle on your head should be!"

If you're black, you know what torture it is to have a Jheri Curl grow out before you get your hair processed and prepped up for the dry, straight, permed style. You got to *wait, wait, wait* until those nasty curls grow out and your roots come in. So you look like Buckwheat for a couple of months, and passing a comb through what is now an Afro can be as painful as losing your virginity.

So of course I waited till my processed, previously ready-for-the-world hairdo grew out before I could process, fry, and distress my tresses again. I believe this was my Don King phase of hairstyles! Yep, quite sure I didn't have any friends during that time. My hair was wispy, damaged, and limp, and I just looked frightful.

So the 1980s were a hairy nightmare in every fashionable sense of the word, but I survived. Although the saga continues, my tresses have now found a style to outlive all trends. Today I wear my hair in braids. The entire braiding procedure takes forty-eight hours. My close friends know not to call and make any plans for me to go out with them then, nor to call during those forty-eight hours, because I am the biggest bitch on the planet as I prepare for divadom.

Now, after I walk out of my hairdresser's home, I feel like I can face the world for the next three months—before I have to go back into hibernation for another forty-eight hours. I feel sexy and confident, my skin glows, and my clothes look better on me. Now it all makes sense when my mom used to say, "Hair makes the woman." She wasn't kidding!

Such a Tease

LIZZIE, PUBLIC SPEAKER, 50

I guess I always wanted to grow up quickly. I saw myself as the runt of the litter, just a girl with two brothers in a very orthodox Jewish home. I never seemed to have my own identity in that house, and I wasn't nurtured in any way but through my religion. I really wanted to be somebody and noted as somebody. So maybe that's why I tried to look a little bit older.

I started teasing my hair in the fifth grade. At the time I also had a mad crush on my teacher. His name was Mr. O'Healey, and he was a very good-looking man, very soft spoken—which I wasn't used to in my household. He was a very gentle soul.

One day I'd had a fight with some guy in the class who was making fun of me and I was crying, and my teacher took me into the coatroom and stood me in front of the mirror and touched my hair and said, "Why are you teasing your hair? You're just a kid. Why don't you stay a kid?" And he started to flatten my hair so that I looked younger. And I never forgot that, because no one ever took that much of an interest in me before in that way. I started to write poetry then too, and he took an interest in my poetry and told me that it was good. I didn't have that in my household . . . I had great parents but I didn't get the nurturing that I needed.

I always wanted to be older because I thought when I was older things were going to be better, and I'd be able to do what I wanted and not have to go to temple every Saturday. Now that I just turned fifty, a very exciting age, I feel my youth coming back. Now it doesn't matter what people are thinking about me, it only matters what I'm thinking about me. I feel so free and young.

Crowning Joy
CARI, WRITER, 30

When I first heard the word *chemotherapy* in reference to me, I was twenty-three years old and sitting in yet another doctor's office in a suburb of Washington, D.C. I had thought, after already living with cancer for two years, that nothing could daunt me anymore, yet my fingers instinctively ran through my hair: shiny, strawberry-blond curls that twirled down my back. I didn't know much about chemotherapy yet, except that it would make me sick and would cause my hair, my favorite part of myself, to fall out.

All of a sudden I couldn't pass by a mirror without staring at my hair. I would glimpse my perfect curls in the reflection of the train window or in the curve of a spoon. Who would I be without my hair? Would I suddenly be ugly? A freak? Some hairless *Star Trek* concoction?

I questioned my doctors as to what I should expect about losing my hair. "Will it at least grow back the same?" I asked. The answer was no. Often it's darker, I was told, and the opposite texture of what it used to be. Would my curly hair come back straight? I recognized how ridiculous I must have sounded—getting all hung up over hair—to the doctor who was trying to save my life. But I wanted him to understand how mine was *more* than just hair—it was my identity, what I considered my greatest physical asset. I wanted to explain about the uniqueness of being a redhead; about all my former boyfriends' self-professed affinity for redheads; about all the compliments I received in the hair salon and from people stopping me on the street: "Is your hair *natural*? The curls *and* the color? What I wouldn't do for hair like that!"

I stood in my bathroom, clipped my hair back, wrapped a scarf around my head, and stared blankly into the mirror. I looked like a mime. This was what I was going to look like: a mime. I tried to prepare for the inevitable day and imagined waking up to find chunks of hair on my pillow.

I had been given the phone number of Wigs on Wheels by another cancer patient. Claire, the owner, arrived in an unmarked car with a luggage rack packed with duffel bags. She handed me back my college sorority photo and the chunk of hair I had clipped from underneath. I had sent these to her so she could see my hairstyle and color. Then Claire set up in my little one-room apartment, spreading her bags on the bed and moving a chair in front of my full-length mirror. She said, "Now, what do you think of this one?"

It was a curly red wig, which she placed on my head. The hair was exactly my color, yet it was short, feathered layers on the top that spanned into bad-perm-frizzy curls. It looked worse than my own worst hair day, worse than my own hair ever looked first thing in the morning. It looked, unmistakably, like a wig, like an old lady's wig.

Claire noticed the terror on my face. She ran a metal brush through the wig. But as she brushed, the curly bottom half grew larger and larger, until the wig expanded into a perfect triangle. I told her, "Please, take it off." Even my own hair, matted to my head, looked better than the wig.

She placed a new wig on my head, with a straight-haired, adorable bob style that hung just above my shoulders, with wispy bangs. I looked good! Then I tried on a frosted blond wig, a brassy blond, a dark brunette, a light brunette, and a short jet-black number. I decided on the straight red one and, in homage to my dark-haired family, a chestnut brown one with long stylish, bouncy layers.

Then Claire pulled out a terrycloth turban she said I would need when I slept. She told me, "Your head will get cold, and it will make your whole body cold. You will not be able to get warm no matter how many blankets you have, unless your head is covered."

Before she left, Claire handed me a little plastic packet of double-sided tape, the kind that men use to keep their toupees on.

Like a little girl playing dress-up, I modeled my wigs around my apartment, brushing the hair over my shoulders, pushing it behind my ears, pulling it into barrettes, back into a low ponytail. I fussed over the new hair for some time, flipping, styling, brushing, just enjoying the motion. When I was done playing, I sat in front of the TV. Alone, in my empty little apartment, I watched The Tonight Show in my wig. I had made peace.

Two weeks after my first round of chemotherapy, I was in the shower when I ran my hand through my hair and found a clump sitting in my palm. I tried not to be sick. I had already cut my hair to a chin-length bob to make for an easier transition. But somehow thinking all this time I could handle it and *actually* handling it were two completely different things.

After my shower, I tried on my red wig. Then I took the shears and chopped off even more of my own hair, leaving it short and close to my head. The rationalization: the less to lose and the less to shove under a wig, which—as of tomorrow—I'd be wearing.

That night my parents drove up from the suburbs and took me to dinner. My dad loved my new cut, and we all joked that it wouldn't last for long. I leaned my head out the back car window and let the wind rip through my hair, taking strands with it. I was laughing then, at the absurdity of such an unnatural phenomenon as losing your hair all at once. In the big scheme of things, in the whole realm of life and death and cancer, what was hair after all? Just dead cells. Just an annoyance one must wash and condition and deep-condition and set and brush and curl and straighten and check and redo, just to start the whole process again the next day. The wig, for a while, was going to set me free from all that. Think of the time I would save. Think of the money I could spend on things other than expensive haircuts and shampoos and conditioners and gels and hairsprays and antifrizz sprays and shining sprays. With hardly a twinge of the sadness I once felt, I said good-bye to my hair for several months and watched it fly by the car window across the expressway.

Before my hair fell out, I had anticipated that every time I looked in the mirror, the image of my bald self would make me angry or sick, reminding me constantly of all I was going through. Surprisingly, my head is nicely shaped; the baldness makes my green eyes stand out. Also, there is a glow about my face—I joke it's probably all the toxic chemicals in me—but deep down I know what it really is. It is inner beauty, rising with all its might to the occasion.

Liquid Lunch
KATIE, STUDENT, 21

When I was in first grade, my best friend, Bethany, was one of those really tiny and tall ballerina types. I was always tall, Italian, hairy, and curvy for as long as I can remember. But compared to her, I was a cow.

We used to talk about what we ate, and it was a competition to see who ate less in a given day. I had heard that Oprah Winfrey had lost a lot of weight by just drinking liquid, so in first grade I used to trade all my sandwiches and food items at lunch for juice boxes. If I didn't trade the food, I would keep it in my lunch bag and keep that inside my backpack.

I was on this liquid diet for three weeks. I don't remember weighing myself, just feeling these sharp pains in my legs and arms and getting excited because I thought that meant it was working. I guess I lost a bit of weight, but I didn't have a lot of weight to lose. I was already a skinny kid. I ended up just looking like a really, really skinny kid.

My parents had to know what was going on, but they never said anything. It was almost like they were happy that they would have a daughter with such a concern for her image. I used to idolize my mother, and she was constantly dieting. We didn't have regular sit-down-together family meals, so it was easy to slip it past them for a while. When my mom finally confronted me, she asked me to eat something, and I remember I told her that I would pig out. But I really just ate a bowl of Rice Krispies while she watched me.

Today weight is on my mind all the time. I'm very tall (five foot ten), so I think I have to be really thin or I look like a giant hulking Amazon creature. I've never had a really constant eating disorder, but I do make myself throw up from time to time if I feel too full.

Atkins My Ass
JOAN, STAND-UP COMEDIENNE, 40

From early, early on, I was into all these fad diets because I was always in competition to get as thin as my mom. My mother went through this phase in her fifties where she was anorexic. I was in high school, and I remember distinctly her saying to me one time, "Hey, I got these new things called Dexatrim. They say you're supposed to take them with water, but there's water in coffee, so why don't we have some coffee and take a Dexatrim?" So we were speeding our brains out and cleaned the entire house, and it didn't dawn on me until years later that, my God, we made a speedball.

My best friend and I came up with many of our own diets. We started with our diets at eleven because we both had Irish birthing figures: we had been bleeding like stuck pigs for a year, already had bras, had sprouted hips. We both had miniature women's bodies. This was a post-Twiggy generation.

Part of the motivation for dieting was boys, although I had already decided that no boys were ever going to pay attention to me. We were tired of being called names. We didn't want to walk down the street and get barked at. We went to a really nasty school district.

By eleven we decided that we were going to lose weight. And our mothers never said, "I'll just give you smaller portions." And

"How's about you eat more fruits and vegetables?" They just went, "Go 'head." They figured we'd be okay because we were looking out for each other.

The first diet was the scrambled egg and water diet. We came up with the diet because we realized we needed at least some protein and we didn't mind scrambled eggs. The water was kind of hard to deal with, but at least this way we were eating something and it wasn't too hard to make. And it was easy to maintain this diet because we would just be focusing on eggs. I think we stayed on it for two weeks. I don't think we lost an ounce, even though we probably ate only once a day. Our bodies, even at that age, were going, "Oh, you're starving me. You know what? *No!*"

We followed that diet with the coffee yogurt diet. Nothing but Dannon coffee yogurt. We were already drinking coffee, so we were drinking coffee and eating coffee yogurt. That diet lasted about a month.

The next diet was the Carnation Instant Breakfast Bar diet. Nothing but breakfast bars, which our mothers added to their grocery lists, figuring, hey, might as well.

The other big thing was the Canadian Air Force exercise book. I have no idea how it got there, but this book was in my house. We'd do all these really advanced gymnastic moves, get sore, and not be able to move for a week. Or we'd ride our bikes on a flat street back and forth. Just completely missing the concept of real exercise, or exercise that you enjoyed. We didn't figure that stuff out until we were in our late twenties.

What we didn't realize back then was that we weren't fat. We were just developed. We were trying to get rid of what were actually decent-looking figures. But because none of the rest of the girls in our class had sprouted tits and ass and everything else (never mind the monthly bloat), there was this trauma.

What somebody should have done was taken us to the Metropolitan Museum of Art and showed us a Rubens.

First Frill: Bras, Designer Jeans, and Stilettos—The Glitter Badges of Womanhood

CHAPTER 4

When Beige Isn't Neutral

DARLENE, PHARMACIST, 36

I don't remember who decided I needed a bra. I probably said something at home about my best friend, Laurie, having a whole drawer full of bras (in sixth grade!). My mother didn't want to miss out on this landmark moment in my life. She threw me into the car and headed off to the mall.

Other girls got to go to the mall, pick out a bunch of bras, and try them on in the privacy of their bedroom. I had to get a bra fitted to my eleven-year-old tits. The bra shop had some fancy European name, the Contessa Shop, that I took to mean "place where they don't have doors on their dressing rooms."

Two old ladies stood at the counter with a wall of bras behind them. I'm sure my mother told them my whole life story while I stared in awe at the melon-sized cups on the top shelf. Somehow I ended up in the dressing room with a couple AA cotton bras. I tried to put the bra on without taking my shirt off. One of the old ladies came over to help. My mom kept saying how important it was that a bra fit correctly. That didn't seem reason enough to let this strange old lady touch me.

I went home with an ugly beige no-frills bra. My mom said beige was versatile. That was the last time I listened to her for the next ten years.

I didn't know the bra was ugly until the next day at school. Laurie, my friend of many bras, and I were changing in the locker room after gym. When I reached for my perfectly fitting bra in the locker, Laurie started laughing.

"Where'd you get that grandma bra?"

She put on her pretty lacy white bra.

I left my first bra in the locker and prayed every night to become a boy. I haven't bought a beige bra since.

Bra = Death

JANE, DEEJAY, 41

I was one of the lucky ones who developed early—in every single possible way, although it was absolutely of no benefit to me. I was the first girl in my school to get a bra. I was in fourth grade, one of those calorically challenged girls who was hanging on to my baby fat. It was the end of the school year, and I was crawling away from the chance to not be picked on. To not be called "Rhino," or "Boulder," or "Bag of Rocks." But then two days before school ended, my mother said to me, "Your T-shirts are not working anymore. We've got to take you for a bra."

To me, this was like my mother saying, "You are a leper, your nose just fell off."

I panicked. I cried, "Please, Mommy, no. Please don't put me in one of those things." Because to me, *bra* was synonymous with *death*. I was in fourth grade, and I didn't want to be different from any of the other girls. I just wanted to be a girl. I was already enough of a weirdo, and for a nerd like me, needing a bra was one of the worst things that could have happened.

So I begged and pleaded, pleaded and begged, all the way to Abraham & Straus, which was so repulsive to me at that point because I also didn't like the idea of shopping at all. And don't draw any attention to me, please, please, please, I begged my mother, just take me to Woolworth's or something. But she takes me to Abraham & Straus, where *everybody* goes.

She drags me in, and I'm like combing the store with all sorts of might and fury, hoping I don't see anyone I know. And I'm hoping my mom is going to keep it really low key. But she turns around in the middle of the lingerie department, and she's got two bras that she's hoisting, and to me it sounds like she's gone on the PA system, because she's screaming, "Which one do you want, Jane?"

I just want to go through the floorboards. I want an earthquake on Long Island right then and there just to suck me down into hell, because that's where I am.

I say, "I don't care, I don't care," and then burst into tears. And my mother says, "I don't understand why you're getting so upset about this," because mothers are always so helpful and full of all sorts of soothing and condolences. Not.

She has to buy the bras as fast as she can, because that's the only way she can get her crying kid out of the store.

They're white, and they have a little red rose with a little blue petal around the outside. I don't even get a training bra. I go right into bra. To make matters worse, the next day is the last day of school, and my mother says to me, "It's going to be really warm out, and I want you to wear your culottes [I hate that word] with your little white shirt."

So my mom puts me in my culottes and my little white shirt and my *white bra*, which is like a neon sign going, *Freak! Freak! Look at the freak!* I do not see this experience as anything that is great. It never dawns on my mother to say, "You know, you're becoming a more of a woman now and this is a good thing." She's from the generation that never talks about anything. Sweep it under the rug, sweep it all under the rug.

So I'm at school and I'm slouching through the day, slouching down at my desk, trying to do everything I can to not be seen. Finally, we're lining up to get out of school to go on the buses, and I'm thinking, "I made it, I made it." And as we're about to walk out the door, Mike Lewis screams out, "Jane's got a bra on!" And everybody either starts laughing or goes "Huh!" And one of the girls just gets so upset because *she* wants to be the first one with breasts. Her name is Joyce Bloom.

I just remember coming home and crying. My mother didn't understand why anyone would make a big deal out of it, and because I was crying she did what she always did when I would get upset at school, which was to say, "Well, if you don't like it, I can send you to parochial school" (where she went, grades K-12). Which would get me to stop crying on a dime. I changed out of my bra and sulked in the dogwood tree that was in our front yard. It was the only tree I could climb.

So that entry into womanhood was not exactly pleasant. I've had so many therapists that have said, "It's not your fault. You have to talk to your inner child and tell her she did nothing wrong. It's beautiful becoming a woman."

But unless you're the girl in school whom everybody loves,

who's genetically perfect, is the honor roll student, is on the track team, is tall and beautiful (yes, I can think of the person I hate to this day who was like that. I want her to be eaten by wolves in Alaska)—if you're not her or one of her friends, you're already an outcast. I wasn't a cheerleader; I had no aspirations to become a cheerleader. I was into rock music, I was a reader, I got along with my teachers. All these things put you into a subcategory of human, according to the popular cliques.

It's only within the last twelve years that I started to realize that all of that stuff was so sad and unnecessary. And it's only within the last six years that I got to the place where I can say, "This is me, this is who I am, and if you don't like it, kiss my ass."

Match Point

MELODY, RESORT HOTEL DIRECTOR, 36

I think one of the happiest times for me concerning a bra would have been the time I realized they sold matching bras and panties. I know that sounds so silly! I must have been in college. Because I remember in high school wearing different-color bras and underwear, but never knew the importance of them matching or that it was "sexy" to have them match. My mother only bought me white bras, and to match white was no big deal. I never thought there ever could be anything fancy or elaborate about the clasps or laces or whatever, until I got out of the house and started buying my own lingerie. That was a happy day for me—I remember coming from Target with my first set. And I was like, "I'm a woman now!"

Now I have this almost aversion to the color white. In my lingerie drawer, I have all my whites on one side, all my blacks on the other. It's a segregated drawer! I have boxes and boxes of lingerie that I can't fit into anymore since I had my child five years ago. It's all floral and printed and really sexy lingerie. Now I have black and white. But I don't think I could wear a black bra with white panties—I just don't think I could do it!

Seeing the Shrink

KATHY, ARTIST, 36

I grew up in the San Fernando Valley. Everyone I went to school with had more money than my family. We were middle class but were always dodging the bill collectors. Everyone else had parents in the entertainment business, so they always had the fashionable things to wear. My mom was a teacher and my dad was a pharmacist.

I had just turned thirteen. Up until that point, my mom always took me shopping at the little girls' shop to buy clothes. Right before I started the eighth grade, all my friends were wearing designer jeans, and I was still wearing generic.

I bought my first pair of designer jeans at a sale in the apartment building where we lived. It took me a week to get up the nerve to ask my mother for the money. I don't remember how much the jeans cost at the time, but it was two or three times as much as the no-name brands. My mom thought it was ridiculous, as most parents do, but the right clothes can be so important for their kids. She finally gave in, and I bought *the* jeans—Chemin de Fer.

I think that you always remember your first pair. You've crossed over and made it. You're not a kid anymore. You feel like an adult, and you're cool. Like that one thing is going to get you accepted into the cool group. Like having the right notebook. There are a number of things at that age where if you don't have them all right, it will separate you from the people who have them all right.

I can't even remember now why my mother and I washed those jeans, but we washed them before they needed to be washed. I think it was my mother's idea to wash them. When I put them on, they didn't fit anymore. You know that feeling where you start to pull them up and they won't come over your hips or your butt? You kind of shimmy them up, but you can't get them zipped. I panicked.

My mother went into rescue mode. This was so out of character for her. I think it was partly because I was so freaked out and upset. She got a pair of pliers and told me to lie down on the bed. She got up on the bed and said, "Suck in your stomach as much as you can." Then she took the jeans and started shimmying them up. She kept saying, "Breathe in," and then she'd shimmy them up. When she got them halfway up, I stood up. As she would pull them up, I'd jump up, so they'd jolt up the rest of the way. And then she could button them. I was squeezed into them for the day. She used the pliers to do the zipper. I don't think I ever unzipped them once during the day—not even to go to the bathroom.

They sure looked good! I remember thinking, and I still feel this way sometimes, when you put on a pair of jeans that are really tight—you put them on and you think, "That looks good!" It doesn't feel good, it feels terrible, but it sure looks good.

Cruel Shoes

MARY, AIR TRAFFIC CONTROLLER, 40

I'm dealing blackjack at a strip club in Colorado. All around me are naked girls in high heels. Believe me, it's a powerful image the first time you see it, especially for a clog-wearing girl like me. I'm not kidding; I'm twenty-two years old and have never worn high-heeled shoes. And all the strippers know it. So they tease me constantly, asking me when I'm going to get rid of those disgusting Birkenstocks.

I decide that it's time to go uptown and buy myself a hot pair of high heels. I'll never forget what they looked like: four-inch skinny little heels, sleek black leather. I am definitely not the most elegant person, but in these heels I feel el-e-gant! Never mind that I'm going to have to deal cards in these four-inch heels all night.

I drive to work wearing my new shoes, get two feet out of my car, and fall flat on my face. I'm sprawled all over the parking lot, and the bouncer comes out to the parking lot and carries me into the bar. We ice my ankle with ice from the bar, and then I go to the emergency room, where the doctor tells me I've sprained my ankle and torn all my ligaments. I really did a number on it, that's for sure.

At the time I thought that high heels were definitely the thing. But then I put them on, sprained my ankle, and went, "What is all this pain about?" I don't know how the strippers did it. I felt sorry for ninety-eight percent of the girls at the bar. Most of them were put up to it by their boyfriends, who would sit there all night in the audience, just to keep sight of their property. I met one girl in the whole time I worked there who had a plan. She put herself through college stripping, and the day she graduated, she quit dancing and opened up a florist shop. But most of the girls thought they were going to be stars.

Now I'm back in my clogs. I wore high heels one other time in my life, and that was at my wedding. But that was it. I'm just not meant to wear high heels. Give me a good old pair of clogs, and I'm happy.

Who's Sari Now?

KAAJAL, GRADUATE STUDENT/SOCIAL WORK, 23

Both of my parents were born in India, they had an arranged marriage in India, and then they moved to Boston, had my brother, and then they moved to New York. I was born in New York, and I've lived my whole life here. My parents didn't really know a lot about the culture, because they were so new to New York. So when they moved into the apartment, they took a lot of advice from the people who lived downstairs from us. They were older, white, Catholic, and very religious people. So my parents ended up sending my brother and me to Catholic school. For my first eight or nine years of school, I was in Catholic school with a lot of very religious white students. So I always felt like my culture wasn't accepted.

Then the first World Trade Center incident happened back in 1993. People automatically assumed that I was from an Arab nation, because of the way I looked or my family looked. So a lot of comments were made. My father used to own a deli at that time, and a lot of the girls in school used to say, "We're not buying food from your father anymore because he probably builds bombs."

When I came out of junior high school and went to high school, I was thrown into a totally different culture. At that time I really questioned who I was. I started hanging out with a lot of black and Latino kids, and that's the kind of culture I took on for myself, in terms of the music, the way I dressed, the way I spoke, the places I went with them. And I was extremely comfortable in this other culture. For many years, people assumed I was Trinidadian or Guyanese; they assumed I was West Indian. And I would always say, "No, I'm Indian." I would just kind of shun it off. It was not something I would press, it was just something like, "Let them believe what they want to believe." Later on down the line, I realized that that was my own way of not having to identify with my culture.

While all this sort of self-discovery was going on, my cousin got engaged. She sent me an e-mail from Boston asking me to be a bridesmaid. I would have to wear a sari, she said, and I could pick whatever color and style I wanted, but it was mandatory for me to wear a sari. So for about three or four months I said, "I'm not doing it. I'm not going to be in this wedding, as much as I want to be, I don't want to wear this sari." My mother would say, "What's the problem? It's not a big deal!" And I would tell her, "It's not a big deal to you, because you wear them all the time."

I didn't know what wearing a sari meant, or what it would mean for me as a woman to identify with a culture that I really didn't wholly identify with. So there was that issue, along with the fact that I'm a little overweight, and when you wear a sari, you have to wear a top that kind of shows your stomach on the side. And my mother kept on telling me, "No, you can wear it another way and you won't have to show your stomach." And finally I said, "You know, I'm going to do it. I'm going to do it for my cousin, and I'm going to do it for myself. I want to be a part of this wedding." So I went to Boston.

I borrowed a sari from one of my mother's friends, because I felt like I would never wear it again, so why spend the money on it? But this sari was beautiful. It was a real dark maroon burgundy color. Now, after wearing the sari, I think they're the most beautiful things in the world because they're so vivid in color. My sari had gold patterns on it, golds, and different greens, and lighter reds. I got dressed in my sari along with all the other women in the wedding party: my mother, my cousin's mother, my aunt, her grandmother, the older women from the family, and the little girls who were going to be the American version of "flower girls." We were all in this one room getting ready.

There's a short story by Edwidge Danticat that has always stuck with me. It's about a mother braiding her daughter's hair, and how through the hours that are spent braiding her hair, like years and years of storytelling, history gets passed down to the younger generations of women. Because it takes so long to braid the hair, it gives the women time to be together and to be in a space that is just their own.

And while I was in this room getting ready, I learned that it's really hard to put on your own sari, unless you're skilled at it. There's a linen skirt underneath and then a bra top, and the sari just comes around; it's just a long, long piece of cloth, and you have to tie it the right way and flip it around your shoulder the right way and use a lot of pins so it won't fall off. A lot of the younger girls, and girls not used to wearing saris, don't know how to do it. So we were in this room with all these women, and it was the first time probably the whole weekend where there wasn't a man around. It was all women. We were all getting ready, and it was the first time I associated that Danticat story to my culture. This is something I can't do by myself, and these women are telling stories. The older women were talking about the first time they were in a wedding, or the first time they wore a sari, or when they got married. And each story was the most amazing story for me to hear, because I was hearing so much about my culture just through wearing the traditional clothing.

This was the first time where I saw something so precious within my own culture. It was at that moment that I said, "This is who I am, regardless of who I identify with outside. These are my people!" I even told my mother, "I can't wait till I put a sari on my daughter for the first time." She started laughing and said, "To think for the last six months you've been saying that you didn't want to do it. I'm really happy that you're in this space now."

So I wore the sari for the wedding. And then for the reception I wore another sari. I loved the way it felt on me. It felt so freeing. You know, when you wear an evening gown, when you have high-heeled shoes on, you feel very restricted, depending on how tight it is; if your bra strap is showing—things like that—you're concerned about it all night. And with the sari on I felt so free. It was so light, in terms of weight. I felt like I didn't have clothes on. I felt like, "This is what I'm supposed to be wearing."

It was the first time I allowed myself to say, "This is who I am." And now I'm proud to say that I'm an Indian woman. Everyone wears henna now, and I keep telling people, "This is where it comes from. This is my culture; this is how we do it."

Well Suited

KELLI, SALES, 22

I don't know how it is at other schools, but everyone at my college is financially minded. Starting senior year, everyone jumps on you with "Have you got your résumé? Did you drop off your résumé at Career Services? Who are you interviewing with?" People start freaking out. Some even have jobs by then—the bankers and financial analysts.

I was a psych major, so I had no idea what I wanted to do; I didn't want to do finance, and I wasn't a math whiz. I played soccer and didn't have time to think about my future until November, when the soccer season was over and I went home for Thanksgiving to relax.

Since companies were starting to come to campus to conduct interviews, I decided it was time to start looking for a suit. My mom's the best person to shop with, because she's dead honest. We went shopping at two different shopping malls and I tried on a million suits; it was a horrible experience. My mom was like, "That one's too short," or "That color looks wrong." I didn't want to get a black or blue one because everyone had black or blue.

We finally found something decent. When we got home, I had to model my suit for my dad, and my mom took a picture. It was a big deal because I'm the baby in the family!

There's a closet in the living room where everyone's stuff is hanging. My brother is married and lives in Georgia, but there's still a coat of his in there. There's stuff of my sister's in that closet, and she doesn't live at home either. And there are coats of my dad's from years ago.

It was odd for me to put my suit in the closet with a windbreaker that was my brother's. I'm sure my sister's worn that jacket, and my dad probably wore it at some point, too—it was just still in the closet. In high school I used to wear a bright blue Adidas jacket with a hood. That was still in the closet for some reason, along with my varsity jacket. All these things were in there. So I threw my suit in there, and I was like, "What am I doing?" Because I just felt so old. In college I had a big long gray coat, and I called it my "big girl coat." Clothing like that symbolizes the transition from college to real life. And it was all hanging in front of me.

It was so hard for me to go to college because I had to leave friends that I'd known since the first grade. It's not like I had a good thing going, but I was good at sports and that took me a lot of places, and it was hard to step out of that. In college I found my niche again; I was in a sorority, the honor society. It seems like as soon as you find your niche, you're asked to leave it. Plus, I'm not good with change to begin with. My parents got new rugs, and I made them save a piece of the old one for me! It was gross, bright orange, but I made them save a piece because you associate things with things from your childhood. I'm very sentimental and traditional. That suit is still a big deal for me because I associate so much with it.

Clearing a Path

All the elements have coalesced: the boobs, the butt, the feathered hair. Now what? I went from longing to look like the bosomy countesses depicted on the paperback covers of my mother's gothic romance novels to wanting to find out what happened to them between the pages (and the sheets!). If the first

transition into womanhood involves acquiring the physical touchstones, a form of self-possession, then the next juncture is about the procurement of others. The yearning is still there, but there is a shift from the "me" to the "you."

The "you" in my case was a boyfriend. I wanted one in the worst way and focused all my ninth-grade attention on the most popular boy in school, Jerry Abrahams. Did I mention that he had no idea of my actual existence, despite my sitting behind him in consecutive homerooms for my entire education up until this point?

He had glorious red hair, an attribute I described in

FIRST FALL: LOVE, OR SOMETHING LIKE IT

p. 101

countless diary entries as being the color of "Indian blood." This attribute caused an obsession so severe, I used to pass notes to my friend Becky in earth sciences class that questioned the color of his other hair. You know, the hair "down there." And instead of doing her homework, Becky used to pen unbelievably filthy stories about Jerry for my benefit.

In fact, through her writing, it was Becky—not a boy, and certainly not Jerry—who taught me about all the "bases," erections, and something she

FIRST FLASH: CANDY FROM A STRANGER—PORN, DIRTY BOOKS, AND OBSCENE PHONE CALLS

p. 128

described as "clumpy white stuff." I never asked her from whom she gained this information, and it took me years to fully understand how she could use a transistor radio as a vibrator, but I count Becky as one of my biggest influences. What I learned from her has never left me, even though her friendship has.

Considering others is self-instructive. Their love, betrayal, and even perversity are held up like a mirror. How can you measure or test another's fidelity if you don't notice the boundaries of your own? How can you hurt someone if you don't know what hurt feels like for yourself? When I was in elementary school, the biggest insult was to point at another girl and say, "I used to have sneakers (or jeans or a polo shirt) like that. Then my father got a job." Ouch—that gibe operates on so many levels, doesn't it?

The stories contained in this section focus on relationships—real and imagined. From heartaches to hard-ons, now is the time to plow through the journey, to whack any obstacles in the way, to avoid disaster, to mark conquests, and to continue onward.

FIRST FLICKER: RECOGNIZING THE POWER OF T&A

p. 152

First Fiddle: Fooling Around and Going All the Way

CHAPTER 5

Gag Gift

SOPHIE, RESTAURANT MANAGER, 27

I wasn't allowed to date until I was sixteen, and then the boy had to come to the house, my parents had to meet him. All that uncomfortable, conservative, midwestern Kansas City family kind of stuff. I'd had a couple boyfriends, but I hadn't even gone down a guy's pants or anything. I had no idea. I barely knew what an erection was.

It was my freshman year in college, and I was dating somebody. And my friends were asking me if I'd given him a blowjob yet. And I didn't even know what that meant. I thought there was this new sexual revolution going on. I had no idea blowjobs had been going on for centuries.

So I had to ask them to explain it to me. I said, "But you have to use the technical terms." Because I don't like saying, "He pressed his dick in my mouth, and I sucked it." And they were laughing because they didn't like saying the word *penis*. We had to have a few drinks before they could tell me how to give one.

A couple weeks after their "lesson," I told my boyfriend that I wanted to give him a blowjob, and of course he was all excited. We were in my dorm room freshman year, and we had just gone out for brunch. It was a typical Sunday morning: brunch, church, and blowjobs! We had eaten some sort of cherry cobbler for dessert. And I remember right after I gave him the blowjob, I gagged and barfed up cherry all over his chest and all over the bed.

He felt bad, because he thought he'd made me do this gross thing. But it didn't affect me or screw up the rest of my sexual life. It was just embarrassingly funny.

Eventually, I learned how to master the gag reflex.

The Writing's on the Wall
RITA, ATTORNEY, 43

I learned everything I needed to know off the walls of the first stall in the first-floor women's bathroom in Brandeis's student union building. The stall was like this giant community bulletin board filled with the most wonderful exchanges of information between young women. It was incredible. You noticed it right away. As soon as you stepped in, you were like, "Wow! Look at this great stuff."

Because it was a ladies' room, a lot of the discussion was about men. And because it was 1975, a lot of the discussion was also about feminist issues. Unlike the wall graffiti in a men's room "For a great time call . . ."—this stuff was like having a philosophical conversation. There was everything on those walls: complete feminist theories, sexual politics, the idea of interpreting people's actions in terms of a worldview—not how some guy is treating you, but how he's treating women in general.

There was a lot of lesbian conversation, which I had never seen before. And a lot of talk about your absolute, inalienable right to have an orgasm. Your God-given right to sleep with anyone you wanted without feeling like a bad girl. (This being a school highly populated by Jewish students, I don't think there was a lot of this virgin-whore thing going on.)

I'd sit there reading the wall; it was just so interesting. The dialogue was all in terms of being a woman, not a girl, and the general advice on the stall's walls was not to be a doormat. Whatever the question, there was no kind of recrimination, no one writing back, "You're stupid" or "You must be a Republican." There were real conversations, and I remember feeling that there was always a spirit of sisterly helpfulness. It was like an anonymous consciousness-raising group for young women who were either too embarrassed or too jaded to admit they didn't know something.

Which is why I felt free to ask this embarrassing, stupid question that could verge on the extreme—or generate pictures. It took me a long time to get up the nerve to post my question. I remember I made some apologetic statement first. And then I wrote my question: "How do I give a blowjob? Please give step-by-step instructions." I think I signed it, "Inexperienced female."

When I got to college, I was one of the few women who were really out to get laid. I think I had kissed maybe two boys in high school. The way I grew up was really repressive, in an extraordinarily dysfunctional family. My parents were both in their forties when I was born, and the generational differences were more pronounced back then. My parents were freakish compared to my friends' parents. I was not allowed to wear pants to school, or a miniskirt (even though I grew up in the era of the miniskirt). I couldn't wear shoes with a heel or slip-on shoes. And these are just small and superficial examples of the fucked-up-ness of my upbringing.

I knew I had to leave home, and I knew that if I didn't, I would die.

At Brandeis, nothing was forbidden. We had officially coed dorms and unofficially coed bathrooms. And there was no talk about sex being bad, or that you could get punished for it. That was all out the window at Brandeis.

It took me all first semester to get a boyfriend, which was just about as long as it took to get up the nerve to post my question. I was too embarrassed to ask my boyfriend how to give a blowjob, but I wanted to be a good girlfriend, and I wanted to do it and do it well. And I was too embarrassed to ask my friends, who I knew were far more advanced than me and I didn't want to look like an idiot. And never in a million zillion years could I have discussed this with my mother.

So I was kind of stuck having this conversation on a bathroom wall.

It took a couple of weeks for someone to respond. It was just your basic instruction—one, two, three, four—no teeth. Ha ha ha. And once I finally got up the nerve to put those instructions to practice, my boyfriend did not know the source of my sudden enlightenment!

Over the course of my time at school, that stall became famous for being what it was. I don't know. Maybe I was very impressionable. I'm not sure what the more experienced women thought of the information exchanged on the walls of this bathroom. I'm not sure if it would have meant a lot to other people.

But then again, there was a community of people who were

writing there, me included. So they must have thought it was an appropriate venue.

Pocket Penguin
KERRY, EDITOR, 25

I'm confident I permanently damaged the poor boy who was my first pants-off experience. Totally shocked at what the merchandise actually looked like up close, I said disgustedly, "Oh my *God*, this can't be the way it's supposed to look!" I promptly buttoned up my prim little shirt and hurried out.

Because, I mean, come on. How ridiculous is that thing? The whole package is utterly absurd! Don't pretend it isn't. I remember thinking the whole way home, "I have *got* to find a way around this." Meaning the male genitalia. Of course, there isn't a way around it—well, there is . . . I went to a small liberal arts college; I figured out The Way Around It, but it isn't a permanent solution for me, so I adjusted.

Now I feel rather fondly toward 'em: they all have personalities, you know. Some are loyal and obedient as dogs; some are more moody and capricious . . . I still think most are terribly funny looking, but in the same way I think that, say, penguins are funny looking. In a cute and sort of vulnerable, goofy way. And yes, I admit that some are downright handsome.

Adult Swim
NINA, NOVELIST, 27

When I was eleven, my mother and I moved in with her boyfriend who had two children, one of whom was a girl exactly my age.

The house he owned was a ranch style with a swimming pool. It was the nicest house I'd ever lived in. We were an instant family. Every day after school my new "sister," Ann, and I would strip off our clothes, put on our bathing suits, and jump into the pool. While I walked on my hands or pretended to be a mermaid, Ann always gravitated to the sides of the pool, resting her chin on the ledge and relaxing. After a few minutes of hanging on the ledge, she'd join me.

One day, as she clung to the side, I swam up as quietly as possible. Her eyes were closed, and her face was contorted into a look I didn't understand. "What's wrong?" I asked. That day she showed me her secret: she was pressed up against a water jet. She said it felt really good. She looked at me very seriously and just said, "Try it."

But I couldn't figure it out. It didn't feel like anything to me. So she took me under her wing and gave me very careful instruction. She told me where to point the jet. She told me to stay there, not to move. Close my eyes, concentrate.

I remember my cheek against the warm, scratchy concrete ledge of the pool. The water that was shooting out of the jet was warm, too, warmer than the rest of the water in the pool. So pressing against the jet was a warm experience, but it was also awkward. I had to hang from the ledge just so, so the stream of water hit at the right spot. For me, this meant hanging from the side of the pool like I was hanging off the side of a building: pressed close, cheek to ledge, dangling dangerously.

The day I found the right spot, the day the jet got me off, I discovered what Ann had been talking about. That had been ecstasy on Ann's face. I felt victorious.

For weeks I had tried, always wondering if what I felt, which was no better than the next sensation, was the thing she raved about. I didn't understand. It felt like all the times I had chased ducks down at the lake: no matter how close I thought I was, I was nowhere near catching one. My first orgasm felt like certainty. There was no mistaking it. It was as unbelievable as having a wild duck in my hands, and as real.

After that day Ann and I always had an after-school poolgasm before swimming and playing like eleven-year-olds. We had no idea that what we were doing was "dirty." To me, it felt as wholesome as cookies and milk.

Within the year my mother broke up with that man, and we moved out. He had been doing too much cocaine and she couldn't handle being a mom to three kids. We were both a little wiser when we left.

Hog Ride
MICHELLE, TRUCK PARTS STOREOWNER, 35

I had just turned sixteen, and was staying at my sister and brother-in-law's house for a month while my dad was gone. Late one afternoon I heard a motorcycle pull up, and in walked a man the likes of which a small-town girl like me had never laid eyes on before. Imagine a tall, dark, better-looking Mick Jagger, with the deepest voice I had ever heard from a white man.

He was a friend of my brother-in-law's from the big city who had come to visit, was about twenty-four, and his second marriage was breaking up. He was so charismatic I could hardly breathe around him. I was unable to stop myself from just making a beeline for him. I stuck to his side all night.

Amused by my behavior at first, my sister became alarmed when he asked me if I wanted to go for a ride. Did I?! Nothing was going to stop me, even my sister's threats of calling the police.

We roared off to a secluded spot down by the river, where we parked the bike and spent the night on the riverbank talking until the sun came up. He did most of the talking, I was too tongue-tied, and what could I talk about that he would be interested in, anyway? I was just a silly schoolgirl who had rarely even been out of my tiny town.

Looking at his full lips, I kept hoping he would kiss me, but he didn't. I had to go home and get ready for school, but we waited until my sister had left for work, then he dropped me off. I was in the clouds, but sad that I'd probably never see him again.

So the next day, I was moping around the house, obsessively thinking about him, when the phone rang. It was *him*, and he told me that he was packing some things and coming back for a while, provided he could find a job.

Oh my God, this was too good to be true! I fantasized—not really about having sex, because I wasn't totally sure what this entailed, but about him being my "boyfriend" and such, and him kissing me.

Soon he was here, taking a room at one of the two motels in town. He came to see me, took me out; seemed interested in me. I had no idea why, but it was flattering, and I just loved it when women's heads would turn to look at him, although I secretly worried that soon he'd meet someone far more sophisticated than me. He also hadn't tried anything with me yet, which made me even more insecure.

My sister was on my back, but I just blew her off. One warm night we made plans to spend the night on the riverbank. God, it seemed like school was twice as long that day. I just knew I was going to "become a woman" that night, and trembled with excitement. Finally, we headed off with sleeping bag (one), radio, and some beer.

It was great. We talked, and danced to the radio. I had a good beer buzz from just the one I drank. We scrounged up enough wood and twigs for a little fire. When it grew chilly, we spread a blanket and put the sleeping bag over us. He pulled me close to him and kissed me (finally!!!), and God I thought I was gonna die right there, it was so incredibly hot, all of a sudden I was filled with all these sexual feelings.

I wanted him so bad, I can't even tell you—I don't think he was prepared for how responsive I was. He explained to me why we couldn't "do it," how he could go to jail and all.

We did take our jeans off, though, but I left my panties on. We continued to make out, and he fondled my breasts, making my nipples hard. Lying on his back, he put me on top of his leg, and with one hand he rocked my body until I came with such an intensity I thought I wet my pants.

At the time I wasn't sure what had happened there, but it sure felt good! He laughed and explained it all to me. I tried to reciprocate with my hand, but I had never seen a penis before, let alone felt one, and I just didn't know what to do! He said it didn't matter, and we fell asleep like two spoons in a honey jar.

Those are good memories. We never did "do it" all the way, and as soon as my dad came back to town, the shit hit the fan, but I'll never forget him.

No Poking Around

STEPHANIE, PORN DISTRIBUTOR, 26

Honestly, I barely remember my first time having sex. I remember before the sex, and I definitely remember after the sex, but the sex itself is a vague memory at best. Most guys say their first time was momentous. Most women say it was painful. The only word that comes to mind for me is "nice." Pretty lame description.

Kevin and I met at Moonlight Beach in California. My friend and I were sitting by a fire, hoping that some cute guys would find us. And they did. They were a little bit older than us, but we could play eighteen for the night, even though we had both just turned sixteen.

Kevin was twenty-one, cute, with a mop of curly surfer hair. He ended up sitting next to me by the fire. We talked about music, mostly hippie music. At that age I was especially attracted to the hippie type. Kevin wasn't really a hippie, but the whole surfer thing was close enough: reggae, joints, world peace, Grateful Dead shows, disenchantment with the establishment, happiness that I didn't wear makeup. He was an open book with all his feelings, I was a sappy romantic, so we were perfect for each other. He was so much nicer than the plastic rich kids I went to school with.

I had three weeks left of my summer vacation, and I spent every night at Kevin's cockroach-infested house. We ate a lot of burritos and talked all night. We really talked about everything, every little experience with the opposite sex, all our embarrassing moments, all our insecurities. I thought I knew everything about him when we decided to have sex. We were both virgins, but we weren't exactly cherishing our virginity. I wanted to go back to school "experienced," and Kevin was twenty-friggin'-one!

After our "nice" sex, I remember thinking that I didn't feel any different—although I apparently felt entitled to look through all his stuff. I started poking around in his room. He had some kind of certificate on the wall—I think it was from some surfing championship. I read the certificate three times, slightly grossed out. Even though we talked about everything, I didn't know his last name until that moment. It was the same last name as mine.

His 'n Hers

CARRIE, LAW STUDENT, 26

I lost my virginity at Teen Adventure, which was a sleep-over camp in Virginia. At the beginning of the summer, my older sister told me, "You should lose your virginity to Donny Rucker." She decided for me. She was very controlling about sex stuff. She said, "Kiss him." And I was like, "Okay, uh . . ." I needed a prompt.

So I lost my virginity to him the summer before I went into my junior year in high school, and very soon afterward I broke up with him to date a boy that I was with for the next two years. I went off to college, and in my sophomore year I meet this girl Patricia who was sitting on the steps of one of the dorms, and she said, "Hey, you're Carrie!" And I responded, "Who the hell are you?" She was all, "I've been looking at your picture for two years. You're Donny's first serious girlfriend; he lost his virginity to you. I've been dating him for the past two years, and we just broke up."

I thought that was kind of weird, her calling me out like, "I know you." We started talking. I lived in this party house that had these big keg parties every Friday and Saturday night. She came to our parties, and we'd hang out. But it was kind of weird because we had both dated Donny, and Donny and I lost our virginity to each other, and she lost her virginity to him. We talked and joked about it.

And one night it was three in the morning, and we ended up in the bathroom upstairs, sitting on opposite sides—it was a huge bathroom—and we were chain-smoking clove cigarettes. The party was over, people had left. We started talking about dating women. I'd never been with a woman before but had always wanted to. We started joking about it and chatting about it. We were flirting and we were really drunk and high. Finally Patricia said, "I gotta go home. It's four in the morning." And I told her, "No you don't, you can stay." And she's like, "No, no, no, I really should go." And I said, "I'm asking you to spend the night, you know." I was pretty blunt with her.

So we go in my room and we're messing around, and it's kind of awkward because neither of us has ever done it before. It's funny, and we're laughing. We end up back in my bathroom brushing our teeth or something, running around the house naked, in this house where everyone else is sleeping, and we're like wandering around naked, going, "Hee, hee, hee!"

We full-out hooked up. And that was the weird thing, because we both lost our virginity to the same guy, and then we both had sex with a woman for the first time with each other.

We ended up hanging out for the next week or so. We hooked up in the library once, in a little study room. She freaked out on me and said, "You're too aggressive! That's what it's like with guys. Women aren't supposed to be like that, women are supposed to be passive."

Poor Patricia—I think it freaked her out. She was beautiful. She was Colombian, had really long black hair, petite. A beautiful woman, but very, very heterosexual. I think it was the Donny thing—she wasn't over him. I was kind of harsh when I broke up with him, and they got together soon after we broke up, and I think he wasn't over me yet. There were pictures of me around, and I was the girl she was jealous of for the two years she was dating him. She showed up at college, and there I was, and it was a weird closure thing for her, I think.

She and I were talking about it that night: "Wouldn't it be funny to lose our virginity to each other because we both lost our virginity to Donny Rucker?" Not in any seriousness, but then we both got drunk enough and decided, "Yeah, okay." I think I talked her into it.

It Happened One Night

HEIDI, MEDIA RELATIONS, 29

It really hit me this year: I may live the rest of my life by myself because I haven't met that special someone yet. I'm beginning to wonder, "Am I doing something wrong?" My friends keep telling me, "You're too picky!" Honestly, at first it kind of made me angry. I was like, "Stop telling me I'm too picky!" Because I would rather spend my life alone than settle. But then I started thinking, "*Am* I too picky? *Am* I preventing myself from really meeting someone or being in a relationship?" At this point I want it so badly! I've never felt like this.

A few months ago it dawned on me that not only am I not having a relationship, I'm not having sex either! So I went out and met somebody on New Year's Eve at some dance club thing. We ended up going out one time. Don't ask me what I was thinking, but I just had it in my head that I didn't care about getting into a relationship with this guy. He was the first guy I'd met in a very long while who was just very good looking. There was this animal attraction kind of thing. When he comes to my door, I just want to jump on him right there. So I go out on this date, and I basically have it in my mind that I'm going to sleep with this person. I've never, *ever, ever* done anything like that in my life. I just thought, you know what, it's time. I didn't do this in my early twenties. It was the single worst sexual experience I've ever had in my life.

I thought that I could do that and be okay with it, but I really wasn't. I don't know what I was thinking; my hormones were doing the thinking really. Obviously there can be no emotional kind of thing with a one-night stand; you don't care about the other person really, it's just about doing it.

But this guy has more of the macho edge going, and I'm just so not used to having somebody move so quickly. It throws me. I want to do it but I don't, and because I'm so unsure, it's a disaster. We're doing it, and my body's all stiff, and I'm thinking, "I don't know this person, I don't really know if I want to be doing this." It is just awful!

The sex doesn't even last because it's so bad. Being the paranoid self that I am, I'm like, "We're using a condom and this spermicidal stuff!" because my fear is always getting pregnant. So we're doing it, and he's like, "Something's stinging!" So that was it. We stop because he says something is stinging. It's laughable because it's so awful. It was very quick but very awful. I thought I would die of embarrassment. I'm sitting there with this guy I don't know, and I'm like, "Okay, not only was I not sure I wanted to do that, but *it wasn't even good!*"

He ends up sleeping over, and I just want him to leave. I want him to be gone! He snores so loud that I can't even sleep in my own bed. I have to move to the living room. The next morning I get up and call my girlfriends, and I'm whispering in the bathroom, "This horrible thing happened . . . and he said it was stinging . . . and what should I do? What should I do?"

So I end up going in the bedroom, and totally still not knowing what I'm doing, we end up fooling around some more. And, oh my God, I can't even believe this, I decide that I'm going to give him a blowjob. So I do, and when I've completed the act, do you know what the bastard does? He gets up and puts his clothes on! Like he's done!

I never felt like such a prostitute in my whole life. I felt dirty, I felt like some kind of cheap whore. I did. Because it's so uncharacteristic of me to do anything like that. And to make matters worse, he doesn't leave. We're sitting out in the living room, and it just is so awkward, and for some reason my mom decides to come over without calling me. Well, she comes up my balcony and is at the door knocking. My apartment is so small, you can see into the living room from the front door. I'm in my freaking lit-tle shorty pajamas, with this guy in my apartment, and here's my mother at the door!

I say to him, *"Oh! My! God! My mother's here!"* I go to the door, and I'm like, "Good-bye. Good-bye." I'm really mean, because I just want her to leave, and she just wants me to introduce her to this guy! I never have been so humiliated in my whole life.

By now this guy is thinking, "This woman is a complete nutcase, because not only is she stiff as a board, but now her mother shows up." So needless to say, he's never called me, and I've never called him, and I never want to.

I thought I could force myself into getting some sex without the relationship thing. And it's just not me. I cried the whole next day. I felt like a tramp. I know people do it all the time, and I don't particularly think there's anything really wrong with it. I wouldn't judge anybody else, but for me, it wasn't good. I felt really bad about it.

Actually, I was out a couple weeks ago, dancing with some friends, and I saw him, and I thought I would puke. Because it kind of hit home that he's kind of out doing the same thing as he was back in January. For him, this is something that he does on a very regular basis.

It was a lesson learned. As much as I want sex, one-night stands are just not in me, you know?

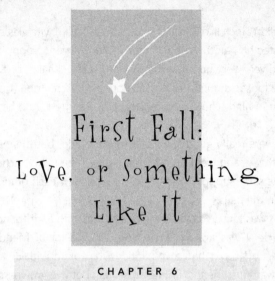

First Fall: Love, or Something Like It

CHAPTER 6

Elvis Has Left the Closet

MONICA, COLLEGE SOPHOMORE, 19

I swear, I will never be able to look at a picture of Elvis with a straight face again. Not that Elvis is particularly amusing, but I can't stop thinking about the boy that loved him. I've known Chris since first grade, and as far back as I can remember, everything I connect to him has to do with Elvis. Like, he always did these impressions. He would curl his lip—this was in first and second grade! Chris wouldn't sing the songs, but he would start talking like Elvis and go, "Hey, hey, hey." It always got a laugh from all of us in the group. He would only dance on occasion, though. I would always bug him to do his impression, and he would hesitate at first, but then he'd always do it.

He didn't look like Elvis. He was short and wore wire glasses. And he frosted his hair this copper color. He looked very preppy, always dressed very, very preppy. Clothes from J. Crew. Khakis, belt, and a tie. He looked straight from a catalog. And I remember one Halloween in high school, he dressed up like a priest. And he fit the part.

We were really good friends in fourth grade, but then we sort of split ways and went on different paths. Then in high school we had the same group of friends so we often saw each other, especially in the halls.

Chris was always single. I never saw him with a girlfriend. And of course, I was always single, too. I had a lot of friends, gay friends, so I never had a romantic involvement with anyone. It was always just friends. I'm heterosexual, but I've grown up to be very open-minded, and my family, my parents, have been very open-minded. Instead of getting Barbie as a kid, I used to get chemistry sets. I've always been the writer, the intellectual. I mean, I liked Enya instead of the Backstreet Boys. I always felt like the black sheep in a way, and I always knew I was a little different than everybody else. It just happened that my friends were a little different, too.

Chris and I always fell into place, just because we were the only single people in the group. He was my obligatory date for all the school dances of high school because we were always without any other choice.

Senior year I started to get the inkling that I had a crush on him. He was always really fun to hang out with, but he did have some idiosyncrasies that were a little weird. The first time I walked into his house, his room was covered with Elvis memorabilia. The clock, the bedspread, everything. It was odd. He had a separate office, with a desk, and I don't know how else to describe it, but it was very officelike. Like, straight out of a movie. He alphabetized all his books and had an inventory of his entire wardrobe, for chrissake!

He was like this little man—that's exactly how I'm picturing him now. A little man, especially because he was very short. And kind of skinny. I'm totally opposite because I'm a bigger woman and taller. Even in my diary, I wrote about people calling us Kermit and Miss Piggy. It wasn't mean, though. It just fit us perfectly in the way we looked together. It was cute.

One time Chris and I were hanging out by ourselves. He took me to the mall, and we were sitting outside eating pretzels, and as I was rambling on about the connection between people's shoes and their sex lives, he said to me—and this should have been a red flag at the moment—but he turned and said to me, "If I was to marry any woman, it would be you." That should have tipped me off right there. I mean saying *any woman*. He definitely specified that. But I didn't think anything at the time. I was ecstatic, and so flattered that somebody had thought that of me. I already had a crush on him. And I had heard some rumors that he liked me, too—from some of my friends—so I didn't really know what else to think about it, except that it was very flattering.

Of course now I look back on that, and I have to laugh. But . . .

On the way home from the mall, I asked him if he was asking me to go out with him. He finally said—and he was very nervous, too—he said, "Do you want me to ask you?" I was like, "Yes." So then it was very awkward. I mean, this was my first boyfriend, and this was his first, well, one of his first, girlfriends. I know this was during my senior year, but I had never had this experience before.

But I should have known. On the day before he asked me out, rumors started to circulate that my best friend Kenny, who is gay, had fooled around with Chris. I didn't believe the rumors at first because of what Chris had told me: "You're the only girl I would ever marry." And Kenny had been known to lie and exaggerate, so I really didn't know who to believe.

But then I started to think: Chris never called me, and only talked to me in school. We were planning on going to senior prom together, but otherwise we didn't hang out much. He would put his arm around me, but he never made any moves at all. He never kissed me. I was disappointed that he never tried anything.

At the prom I had literally grabbed his hand to hold hands with him, but it was very awkward, and he really didn't make any moves otherwise. And at the after-prom camping party, which was at my house, I got a little tipsy. We were sleeping in the same bed together in the camper, and I went to kiss him, and he acted like he was totally asleep and basically pretended to be dead. And I knew he wasn't. So I just turned over and went to bed. And people were hooting and hollering, thinking that we were . . . whatever. But we weren't. I think that's when I knew that Chris was, in fact, gay.

After that night Chris didn't call me. He just disappeared for two weeks. When I finally did get hold of him, weeks later, I asked him straight out, "I've been hearing these rumors, and I just really want to know: are you gay? Because I really don't want to be lied to." He started to cry as he said, "No, no, no!" to me. A short time later I found out he had been in Bermuda for those two weeks and "forgot" to tell me. I broke up with him right then and there.

That's when I realized he had used our "relationship" as a cover-up so he could deny his homosexuality.

My heart has been broken by at least eight men, and they've all been gay. I feel like it's more of a sad destiny than a mere coincidence. I figure that any guy who gives me any attention must be gay, and my gay-dar is so good now that I can spot 'dem buggers from a mile away. I haven't had a "boyfriend" since the whole incident with Chris, but I'll be sure to do a background check on him before I do.

There has been a good thing that has come of this, however. I have gained some of the best friends I could ever ask for, all except for Chris, who I still don't talk to, for obvious reasons.

Dance Lessons
PHYLLIS, ATTORNEY, 45

I was an athlete in high school and a really smart kid. I went to an all-girls Catholic school in Philadelphia, and we would routinely pillage the ranks of our "brother" school for dates to these awful high school dances. I grew up around boys, played basketball in the driveway with my three brothers and all their buddies, but the one kid who had my heart from the time I was ten was named J.J. He was the best friend of one of my brothers. God, he looked just like JFK Jr.

J.J. treated me like a little sister, but I still kicked his ass at whatever game we played. Whenever he'd come over, I'd refuse to pour him a drink from my fridge, or I'd call him "Football Head" like everyone else did—but man, did I lose so many heartbeats to that boy. Here I was, physically strong and steady, getting A's in school, but I was totally confused as to why boys weren't interested in me. I found out at the Harvest Moon Ball.

This was one of those pitiful dances that occur every fall, when the gym was turned into a haystack or something. I screwed up my courage in my junior year and asked J.J. to the ball. Of course he said yes—it was the polite, JFK thing to do.

When he picked me up that night, I had convinced myself that I would let him have his way with me, whatever that meant. He was wearing a blue suit, looking absolutely gorgeous. And I'll never forget what I wore: black high-heeled shoes with big bows, a pink top that was made out of crinoline, a purple miniskirt, and a choker just like Cher used to wear. Remember, this was the 1970s.

I was sixteen years old, and for the first time I wanted to feel female and feminine and I really wanted J.J. to be attracted to me. But as we danced beneath the crepe paper to "Stairway to Heaven," my eyes wandered across the room to Lana Kane and her boyfriend. God, he was so smitten with her! Her long hair swung just like a shampoo commercial, and her legs were endless. Lana was a lousy student and didn't know anything about sports, but there was her boyfriend, practically having sex with her on the dance floor while J.J. and I danced miles apart. As the song came to an end, he looked straight through my head, straight through to Lana.

It was the first time I realized that I wasn't going to be the kind of girl to get the guy. It hardened my sixteen-year-old heart, and it's kept me from sustaining a relationship. I've been married and divorced twice—to total narcissists. I've allowed men to look right through me because I felt so invisible. I've waited for a man to validate me, to tell me I was pretty, to hold up that mirror.

I now know this is just me trying to get my father's attention. He was cold and distant, unavailable to me in so many ways. But he's dead now. I think he's finally seeing me.

I woke up this morning, thinking about this time in my life. I realized that I've been the invisible woman for forty-five years! But I am not invisible. I'm here.

Tough Love

BARBARA, PUBLIC RELATIONS, 44

I was a sixteen-year-old girl, a sophomore in high school, living in an upper-middle-class family in the heartland. Just a young girl who played three varsity sports, was in the National Honor Society, the second oldest of four girls, with a dad who went to work every day and a stay-at-home mom. So to the outside world, we pretty much had a perfect family. And really in a lot of ways it was very, very ideal.

I had once been the type of girl who was always very outgoing and confident, but I never really had a lot of interest in boys. I mean, I knew they existed and I was attracted to them, but none of my sisters ever dated, and there weren't a lot of boys around the house.

But then this older guy came into my life. Sammy was four years older than me. I met him through my friend Trish. We were all at a party, and Sammy flirted with me. I had boys flirt with me, try to hold my hand, but I just wasn't interested. But this guy was tall, blue-eyed, and blond; had graduated high school already, was a good athlete, was going to college, and also had a part-time job. And interestingly enough, my dad was a big golfer and used to play every day—and this guy was a scratch golfer. He had a zero handicap. So in my mind, this guy was just like my dad.

A few weeks after that party, I was invited to the junior prom. I was only a sophomore, but my friend Mike was a year ahead of me, and he invited me. Trish was also a junior, and she asked Sammy to go with her. So we all went together—but just as friends. We got to the prom, and as I was getting out of the car on my side and as Sammy was getting out on his side, I looked over the top of the roof, and Sammy looked at me and mouthed the words, "I love you." I had never had anyone before say that to me. And that night at the prom, he said to me, "I want to go out with you, I want to ask you out."

So we started going out. He was a doer. We'd go places together, out for walks, to the park, sporting events. And he also was the kind of guy who constantly sent cards, notes, and letters. In a way, he was almost setting me up for the brainwashing.

Sammy loved the Beatles and was always playing their albums.

When John Lennon was coming to town, Sammy had said to me, "John Lennon is going to be on Channel Six. Let's go down and see him." There weren't a lot of people at the station, so we got to meet him. All I can remember is looking at John Lennon and thinking, "This is the ugliest man I've ever seen in my life. What is the big deal?" But Sammy was just blown away.

The first time he kissed me was around a month after the prom. He was over at my house. We had a beautiful home with a pool, and because I was Irish Catholic growing up, there were always priests and nuns hanging out around the pool, drinking Chivas.

It was a warm summer night, and I walked Sammy out to the driveway. We were standing side by side, leaning against a red Dodge Dart. And he leaned down to give me a kiss. It was my first kiss. I felt my whole body go flush, and it seemed like rockets were going off in my head. I knew that Sammy had gone out with a lot of women, and I looked at him and said, "You're disappointed." I was afraid it was so obvious that I was clueless. And I think that in that moment, he saw me as this perfect, sweet, innocent human person. He knew that I had never been touched, and I think that at some level that was really powerful for him. That he could mold me and create me into whatever he wanted me to be.

I was with him every day. He was very much a part of my life. My parents liked him, too. He would have lunch with my mom while I was at school, or he'd play golf with my father.

It was a few months before Sammy gave me some alcohol. I never drank alcohol before, but it progressed to the point where I started to drink and lie about it. And I'd never, ever lied in my life. And I lied for a year. I remember I was playing summer league basketball, and I had gotten drunk before a game. And my girlfriends knew about it. They were very much aware of what was going on. They alerted my mom. But she didn't do anything. I had always been so honest that everybody believed me. And Sammy was so charming and personable; he was like a Prince Charming, so nobody suspected him either. It was like a one-act play.

Pretty much all the time now, Sammy was telling me he loved me. He loved me, he loved me. And one night my parents were out, and he came over, and he raped me. And as he was on top of me, raping me, he was screaming, "This is love. This is what love is." I remember just literally dying. Coming out of my body and watching this happen, and really just dying. I ceased to exist. I know that I've had two lives: before sixteen and after sixteen.

Being raped implied a lot of different things. First of all, I wasn't a virgin anymore in my mind. The philosophy in my house was that you grew up, you fell in love, and you got married. And then you had sex. So I thought you married the person you had sex with. When this rape happened, I felt like I allowed it to happen and I had sealed my fate. I'm done. My life is over. This is how it's going to be.

Shortly after the rape, we went to a baseball game with a friend who had graduated with Sammy. For some reason—I don't know, maybe I got angry—I said, "I'm going to go wait in the car." After a while Sammy came looking for me, and when he found me, he had this panicked look on his face, like he couldn't find me. I was standing next to the car, and he came up to me and grabbed me by my neck. Then he punched me in the face. That was the first time. It continued for a year.

Every time he would hit me, he would cry and say he was sorry. But it escalated to the point where he would say, "If I come to your school, and there's a boy sitting next to you in class, I'm going to kill you." Even if I looked at a guy on a billboard, like the Marlboro Man, he would go into a rage.

When he wasn't threatening to kill me, we were having sex. Or rather, he was having sex with me. Sometimes up to seven times a day. Sometimes he'd come to my school and say, "Barbara, let's go have lunch." In the meantime, I was maintaining an A average, playing varsity basketball.

I got out of the relationship at the end of my senior year. I was so afraid that something would happen to me and no one would know why, I wrote a letter and taped it to the bottom of the desk I used in my father's office, where someone would find it if I disappeared.

Finally, what happened was, we were in the car and this Gordon Lightfoot song came on the radio. Part of the song that goes, "I don't know where we went wrong, but the feeling's gone." And I looked over at him and said, "It's over." I was so afraid that he would hurt me. I ran out of the car and ran in the house and told my mom everything.

She told me, "Get over it."

I know that my mom was aware of what was going on. She once took me to the doctor with a broken cheekbone when Sammy knocked me out for refusing to burn my sophomore yearbook. (Some of the guys had written things like "It's been nice knowing you" or "Hope to see you over the summer" and then signed their names "Love, so-and-so.") At the time I told her I got hit in the face with a hockey stick, but she knew. There were a lot of adults around who saw this happening and didn't intervene. To this day, I don't know why.

I've always been a person to stand up for other people. This is the one time in my life I didn't stand up for myself. And I try to understand why. I look back on this incident, the lying there, the coming out of my body, and it's almost like watching a play or a movie. And as I'm watching this happen, I'm thinking, where are all the people? When is someone coming to help me? But the truth is, no one came. I guess it was just survival that I got out of it myself. And the sad way this has impacted my life is that I believe that the only person I can count on is myself. That has carried me through my life. I want to believe and trust people. And I think I do, but on a certain level, I'm waiting to be disappointed.

Self-Love

JILL, NURSE, 31

I had this very tender relationship with a woman. We were both dating men, but then we wanted to be with each other. This was in college, of course! In Nebraska.

She kind of looked like me, a little bit! She wasn't really, really feminine, she had a really nice smile, really long straight brown hair. She wasn't into frat parties or real social things. She was just quiet and gentle and relaxing.

We'd spend long days in bed with each other, just rubbing each other's head and back. We were very gentle with each other. I remember being shy. We didn't want anyone else to know about our relationship.

Things became sexual later. But we still kind of kept it between us. We didn't think either of us was gay. It was fine if we were, but we were both attracted to men. We just loved being with each other.

We spent a whole semester together like that, and then we had to go home for the summer. We kissed each other good-bye and parted. I think it would have ended naturally. We spent this nice time exploring each other and feeling good with each other. But I think in the end, we weren't gay, so we didn't end up committed to each other for our lives. Actually, one night when I went to a party with her (planning on going home with her), I met my husband!

I have no idea what she's doing now, if she's married or not. But I still have nice, tender memories of her.

A Winning Hand

DEBORAH, RETIRED KINDERGARTEN TEACHER, 78

The first time I met my husband, it certainly wasn't love at first sight. I was thirty-nine and was working at an exciting job in Manhattan, fund-raising for a major company, living in my own apartment, busy with interesting friends—just enjoying what I thought was a terrific life. I frankly didn't think that I needed a man for anything, and at my age, I didn't think I was going to find one anyway.

I had come home to New Jersey for a visit, and an aunt of mine insisted that I come over to her house for a game of bridge. Well, I had just washed my hair and didn't want to go out. But my father was going over to play cards, and he was very interested in having me accompany him. I couldn't understand why he and my aunt were so persistent, and my mother said, "There's probably some man over there they want you to meet."

When we got to my aunt's house, there were four people sitting around the table playing bridge, and I was introduced to a young man. Well, if I had been one of the fifty-two cards, he might have looked up. I got absolutely no reaction from him whatsoever.

He did call me a few nights later. We went out for dinner, and the rest is history. I guess he kind of grew on me. We were married for thirty-four years before he died, and I wish I had thirty-four more years with him.

My One and Only

MARINA, TECHNOLOGY PRACTICE DIRECTOR, 27

I met my husband, whose name is Joe, back in 1991 when the first George Bush was president. He was fifteen and I was sixteen, and we were both at the same spring break party. It really was one of those cinematic moments where you see each other from across the room and your eyes meet and you just gravitate toward each other.

I called him a couple nights after I met him to invite him to another party. This was when I found out he was only fifteen because I said, "Do you want to come pick me up before the party? Maybe we'll go to dinner or see a movie or something."

And he said, "I can't pick you up."

I said, "You *can't* pick me up or you *won't* pick me up?"

He said, "I just turned fifteen and a half and just got my driver's permit."

I'm like, *"What?"* Because when you're a sophomore in high school, you just don't think that boys who don't have their driver's licenses are very cool.

And he's like, "You're going to have to come get me because I'm not old enough to drive."

The first time we kissed, he missed, even though he'll say that I turned my head. And when he asked me to be his girlfriend, he wasn't even that good at it. What happened was, I said, "My aunt was over today, and she'd like to know if we're boyfriend and girlfriend. You know, are we serious and stuff?"

And he looked at me and said, "Okay."

I said, "Okay what?"

And he said, "Okay, you can be my girlfriend now."

Pretty much everything with him was my first: first kiss, first boyfriend, first time. It's a typical first-time story. He was just a guy who had been trying to "get some" up to that point and kept failing, because you know, when you're fifteen, you're just not that slick. Then we finally did it; everything seemed to be working properly. And he was all happy, but I was like, "That was the worst thing ever! That was painful!" I remember saying, "Never again is this ever going to happen between the two of us. Never, ever, ever are we ever doing that again!"

I think we did it again probably a week later!

Joe and I got married ten years to the day from when we started dating. One reason why I think we've been able to survive this long has a lot to do with our backgrounds. We both grew up in Las Vegas. We're both only children. Both of our fathers are American and come from blue-collar families. And our mothers are both ethnic—his mother's from Iran, and my mother's from the Philippines—so they both have thick accents and they don't understand American culture that well.

Being only children, I never had to learn to share, and he never had to either. If I need my space, or I'm selfish with something, he understands why, and vice versa. Other people who have brothers and sisters don't understand me. They think I'm being selfish when I'm not being selfish. I'm just looking out for number one, because that's all I've ever had to do.

I haven't really met a lot of people who are only children and married. It's so sad too, because if we have kids, they're not going to have aunts, uncles, or first cousins either, and I'll never have a niece or nephew, and neither will he.

Kept in Suspense

LIZ, LAW STUDENT, 33

My mother thought I needed to be outdoors more, which I did. I was doing this kind of new wave thing, with the spiky hair shaved up in the back, and yellow lipstick, and my mother thought it was awful, which it was. So she sent me away to Wyoming to this wonderful science camp. We'd canoe, study forest ecology, all sorts of things. It was really fascinating. The counselors took away our razors, so we got really hairy. We were backpacking, so we couldn't take anything extra. We couldn't take deodorant or anything like that. It was all natural. And it was wonderful.

I fell in love with this total hippie boy from Wyoming who ignored me most of the time. He had long strawberry-blond hair, he was really tall, and he was pasty white. His name was Mike, and he was totally aloof. I was fifteen; he was seventeen.

There weren't that many kids in the group, maybe ten or fifteen, and we'd go out on these little backpacking adventures. There was one night we had all gone skinny-dipping down at the hot spring, and we decided we were going to get drunk. Somehow we got grain alcohol, stopped up the cabin sink with half a banana, and made this awful drink. Drank it, got really drunk, and then we were just talking about sex, and so the group decided that I was going to have sex with Mike.

Mike first said that he would do me, and then he would do my friend. Which was awful, but I was in love with him, so I thought he at least had some feelings for me!

We had had way too much to drink by that point, and I remember I was trying to be responsible at the same time. I don't know why I thought I could do this at fifteen, but he didn't have a condom. And I said, "What are we going to do if I get pregnant?"

And he said, "We'll buy a little pink house." It was so stupid! But basically he could not stay hard enough to break my hymen. There was a lot of poking about, but none of it was very sexy.

Eventually, he asked me to give him a blowjob. I had no idea what to do. This was made even worse by the fact that I had cotton mouth. So he's instructing me on technique, because he was seventeen. I just remember him saying, "Suspend the testicles." Which meant he wanted me to hold them in my hand.

Now keep in mind, this is an old cabin, and everyone is trying to go to sleep, and the walls are really thin. There's this guy on the other side of the wall, and he's going, "Will you just do it already?!" And the whole time, going through my head is, I really like this guy . . . this is really unpleasant . . . surely it's got to be better than this.

I'm pretty sure the blowjob was unsuccessful. I just finally quit and left.

That was it. I never fooled around with him again. After the summer, we wrote letters to each other for a while. They weren't lovey-dovey or anything like that, just sort of what-are-you-doing kind of letters. He had really bad spelling.

Better Late Than Never

ABBY, SOCIOLOGIST, 27

I've dated a lot of jerks; in fact I've always seemed to prefer them over nice guys. I guess it's that whole challenge fetish. Finally, at age twenty-seven, I like a guy who's really nice, likes me, and treats me well. And you could say it's mutual. You could also say that it's my first real relationship.

I guess I'm a late bloomer in terms of romantic development. I've dated lots of interesting characters but no one that held my interest—or had me hold theirs—for long enough to get serious. But Ben says all those things I've always wanted to hear and does all those sweet things I've wanted other guys to do. He does my dishes! Which is good, because I'm not very domestic. He may be just a scrawny Jewish dork to others, but to me he's a Superhero, a true renaissance man.

See, I always wondered how I would find someone who meets all the criteria—Jewish, smart, funny, nice, *modest* (that's very important—not pretentious or full of themselves), shares my interests, like running, and has an appreciation of cultural activities.

Ben's all that and more! He's a really good artist and paints me pictures when he's bored at work. He likes going to museums, he teaches guitar, has run a couple marathons. He doesn't care about watching football! And he cooks. I just can't believe there is someone like him.

Sometimes my sister asks me if he's gay, which is funny because that's basically what I've always wanted—a straight gay man. I also always wondered if it was possible to find both comfort and passion in one person. At first I wasn't sure about the passion part—wasn't sure if I was attracted to him. We spent the first month just hanging out as friends and getting to know each other, which I think is good because in the past I always got physical too fast and then couldn't relate to the person on a friendship level.

Last weekend I finally heard those three words I've always been dying to hear and sometimes was tempted to utter: I love you. And he meant it. And so did I, when I said it back.

When Food Is Love

KELLY, ACTRESS, 30

I don't cook at all. I don't bake. When I "make" cookies, it's usually from a mix, and that hasn't been in about fifteen years. But this year, for the first time ever, I baked a cake. I did this because my boyfriend said, in passing, that one of the nicest things anyone had ever done for his birthday was to make him a cake. He said it was nicer than any present or gift. He even had another friend back this up—"Isn't that the nicest thing a woman can do for you?" I swear he wasn't dropping hints.

His birthday was a couple months off, but the proclamation was enough to send a panic through my mind. Mind you, this was over a couple drinks, at about two in the morning in a bar in New York. So I know he wasn't thinking, "Go out and bake me a cake." This was about March, and his birthday was in June, but I stored this away in my brain and began to mildly obsess.

I must admit that part of the reason I was prompted to do this was that the person who had made the first cake for him was his old girlfriend, a woman named Mari Felix, from Valencia, Spain. I had always imagined her to be very beautiful, and Spanish of course, *and* she had her Ph.D. So there's one more thing that she does—she bakes cakes! I thought, "Oh no, here I am trying to measure up to Mari Felix from Valencia again."

So I started asking friends I knew: "Do you know how to bake a cake that's not from a box?"

I looked in ladies' magazines like *Redbook*, conferred with friends, got a couple recipes that proved to be way beyond my means. I even asked the guy at Macy's, where I ended up buying one of those Bundt pans (which I think helped make the cake look very impressive).

Finally I got a recipe for a chocolate cake. I thought, "Everybody likes chocolate." I thought it was within my doing, and once I had this Bundt pan, I thought I was all set. As I began to make it, I started thinking, "What if it doesn't turn out okay? Maybe I'll make it a little richer than the recipe calls for. If it's not going to be good, at least it'll be rich." So I added more chocolate in the form of chocolate chips and chocolate pudding mix. I also got fancy and added some sour cream. And I made it. I baked a cake. It came out really rich. But my boyfriend did like it. He actually ended up freezing some of it because he said he wanted to save it for later.

I learned through this experience that I'm really in love—I must be. And I must be pretty intimidated by old girlfriends. I think I'll do it again, God willing, if we're still together next birthday. I'll make him another birthday cake. Yeah, I'll do it again, because I'm not afraid.

First Fascination: Idolatry, Puppetry, and other Forms of Worship

CHAPTER 7

Ideal Worship

CHRIS, GRAPHIC DESIGNER, 54

I was nine years old and living in Florida with my grandmother when she suddenly died. My parents were in Europe, so my mother's sister and her husband had to come down from New Jersey and take care of things. They took me back home with them, and I spent about a month in New Jersey living with my aunt and uncle and my three cousins.

My cousin Molly was about six years older than me, and she was my total idol, my first idol ever. She used to take advantage of that. I didn't care, hell no! Because she was the one who used to sneak me into tennis tournaments. She knew where the hole in the fence was. We would just sneak in, spend the day, flirt with boys, eat French fries, and watch a little tennis. But mostly we were just getting away with stuff. She was always getting away with stuff.

Molly did all the cool things. She drew fashion designs, and they were awesome designs, beautiful stuff. She gave me my first bra; it was hers, and I got to have it. She gave me all of her old prom dresses, which I could dress up in. She was just really nice to me, she treated me like a grown-up instead of a little kid.

Now she's an attorney for some insurance company in South Carolina.

Puppet Love
MEGAN, ACCOUNT SALES MANAGER, 27

I wanted to be just like Miss Piggy when I was five. She was just so glamorous. Her clothes were decadent, she was an actress, and she had that whole diva attitude. I thought she was beautiful. I think I might have been in love with her.

To me, she was a real person. I remember putting on a puppet show with my friend Heather, and she had a Miss Piggy puppet and I couldn't believe it. I didn't think you could actually go out and buy your own. And I thought this puppet was beautiful. Piggy was wearing her long purple dress and opera-length gloves, with blue eye shadow and pearls. I hid it under my bed, and my friend screamed and cried because I refused to give it back. It was a bitter fight. Finally, I traded my Kermit puppet and Ralph (the Muppet Band piano player) puppet for her.

Even at a young age, I recognized how in control Miss Piggy was. She was so dramatic and so over the top, but it never brought her down. Plus, she was one of the only women on *The*

Muppet Show, so she was definitely the star. I identified with that, because I was always the center of attention in my family.

And I like how she manhandled Kermit. I was always into shorter, skinnier, more passive guys. I tried to do what Miss Piggy did to Kermit, which means I would often think, "What would Miss Piggy do in this situation?" To me, she was the precursor to the What Would Jesus Do? movement.

Miss Piggy taught me not to be overly concerned with my weight or how I look. It's really a lesson I've carried with me my whole life. About four years ago, when she was the spokesperson for Baked Lays, I remember being really annoyed when I saw the commercial. I thought, "Right, like Miss Piggy would ever eat Baked Lays." She would have gone for the calories!

On the Road—Beats Reading

CAROLE, HIGH SCHOOL ENGLISH TEACHER, 55

I graduated from high school in 1965 in New Jersey, then immediately went to college in Iowa, where everything and everyone was ten years behind. Hanging from the ceiling over the door of the art department was this huge banner that said, "The ugly can be beautiful; the pretty, never." It was a quotation from Paul Gauguin, although I didn't know it at the time. That banner had such an impact on me! Seeing it every day, thinking about it . . . little did I know, it's a tenet of modern art.

I went home for Christmas, and my mother bought me this cute little white fake fur jacket and a cute little rabbit's fur hat that tied under the chin, and I went back looking like this cute little snowball. But over Christmas vacation I also happened to read *On the Road* by Jack Kerouac, and it changed my life. And I got this idea I wanted to hitchhike some place. But it was Iowa and it was January and we had only a weeklong semester break. I was staying at my boyfriend Dennis's house, who was also from New Jersey. I said, "Want to hitchhike someplace?" And he said—I remember what he said—"Hitchin' with a chick? Cool!"

So without even looking at a map, we decided we wanted to hitch to Denver, because we wanted to see where Jack Kerouac hung out. We actually thought we could hitchhike from Iowa to Denver in the winter and be back in a week! But maybe, we thought, we'll hitch to Kansas City first. And of course, because we didn't bother to look at a map and find out that Kansas City is completely in the opposite direction of Denver, it would take us totally out of the way.

Dennis decided that if I traveled dressed up as a boy, I wouldn't get harassed. And I have a picture of it; somebody took a picture from our dorm window. In it, I look like a big puff in this big huge down jacket that belonged to his roommate. And I had some boots and I had my hood up. I looked like a lump.

We set off at night with a huge duffel bag full of canned food, which we wound up dumping in a ditch after about an hour of walking down the highway with it. It took us forever to get a ride. It took us two days to get from Iowa to Kansas City; it should have taken a few hours. We got picked up by the Missouri State Police, and I, of course, didn't bring my identification and I looked really young and they didn't believe I was over eighteen, so they took us into the police station and called the college and had to verify that I was a student there and that I was over eighteen. Then everyone at the college, which was really small, figured that we must have stolen a car. And they couldn't wait for us to get back and find out if we were going to be arrested. They thought I was pregnant. All these things—if you're hitchhiking with a guy, you must be corrupt and evil and sinful.

So we finally got to Kansas City and wound up in this horrible,

horrible hotel with roaches and holes in the wall and a bathroom down the hall. All we had enough money to do was go to see *The Sound of Music* and then hitchhike back out.

The point is, we were *so* happy—maybe it was a manic episode—but we were so happy to be in these horrible places, doing these ridiculous things in the middle of winter, and freezing our butts off. We even got a ride in the back of a pickup truck when it was sleeting and we were screaming and we were happy. Because it was like we'd broken out of this 1950s mold and we were going to be like Jack Kerouac and we were going to be tough and cool and travel around, and that's when I gave up wearing that stupid white bunny coat.

When we returned to college, I was called into the dean of women's office. This dean was named Betty, and she was about six feet tall and very oppressive and very conservative, and she kind of loomed over me and folded her arms in front of her and said, "The last time girls were caught hitchhiking in this school, they were expelled." And they had only hitchhiked to Des Moines!

Dennis had been called into the dean of men's office and had explained to him that we weren't having sex and that it was all very innocent, and somehow the dean of men managed to talk Betty into not expelling me.

After the hitchhiking debacle, there was a lot of gossip on campus and people thought I was really wild. But I knew there were a couple girls who were sneaking out of the dorms and having sex. And I was just sneaking out of the dorms to go for walks and write poetry!

That's when I started wearing ugly old clothes, or somebody's dad's army pea coat, and not wearing makeup. I didn't want to be cute anymore. I looked like Sally Field in those days, and it was kind of hard—people used to call me "Gidget." I think it was the beginning of feminist ideology within me. That's why that banner in the art department made such an impression on me. I realized that it was more important to be who I am, and more important to have the life of the mind, than it was to be a cute little girl and try to find a husband.

On a High Horse
JENNA, PENSION ADMINISTRATOR, 51

I swear, there have never been any photographs of me by myself. I'm always holding a turkey, holding a chicken, a rabbit, a stray cat. I was crazy about animals. I don't know why I loved them so much, but I did. Sometimes more than people.

When I was fifteen, I wanted a horse more than anything in the entire world. Now, I know what they say about girls and horses. That there's some sort of sexual component to it, but I don't know what that's all about. All I know is that I wanted a horse as much as I wanted to live.

My father was not happy about it and said there was no way he was getting me a horse. He said that I was sure to get into boys, and then I'd lose interest in that horse pretty quickly. He was set against the idea.

But my mother thought different. She was the typical steel magnolia southern woman. Very nice on the outside, but don't cross her. My mother was beyond her times in that she was very emancipated. Especially when it came to my father!

She used her own money to get me my horse, Sally. The day I got my horse, well, I have never been so happy in my life. Isn't that sad?! That day remains the happiest in my memories. Sally was so sweet. I learned how to show her, brush her, groom her, and feed her. I loved everything to do with having my horse. Isn't that terrible? I can't think of any other first, other than getting my horse. Nothing else compares to that feeling of pure happiness.

I had Sally for twenty-three years before she died. She had

stopped eating, and I had been sitting next to her when she fell to the ground. I called her name and her ears perked up and then she died. I cried my eyes out.

Lifetime Subscriber
EVELYN, PHILANTHROPIST, 75

I discovered *The New Yorker* magazine, and it changed my life. I was waiting for the subway, looking at the magazines. I wasn't interested in any of the home or family magazines, because I was just sixteen years old. And then I saw *The New Yorker*. I had never seen that magazine or heard about it, so I bought it and started reading it, and I fell madly in love with it!

I started getting it every time I rode the subway. I had to save my money and get it! My father saw me reading it and said, "Do you like that magazine?" And I said, "Yes, Daddy, I like it very much." He asked me where I got it, and I told him at the newsstand. So he said to me, "I think it's terrible that you're paying newsstand prices. I'll get you a subscription." He sent away for that subscription when I was sixteen, and he got it for me until he was eighty-six, when he died. But I still get it.

The New Yorker opened my world to literature and learning. In my family, we were expected to go on to a higher education, and *The New Yorker* was the beginning of mine. I didn't know about writers until I started reading their stories, and they were so good. The short stories were so wonderful. I loved "Talk of the Town," and all those tiny little remarks at the bottom of the page. I thought that was so clever! I used to read it from cover to cover.

The Harvard Lampoon used to take over an issue—they don't do it anymore—and they made fun of everything. At first I didn't understand anything, but I stuck with it and kept reading. And it eventually dawned on me that it was a parody. Then I enjoyed it so much!

Oh, and the cartoons! I fell madly in love with them. Steinberg . . . ah! And Peter Arnaud! All those famous cartoonists! I'd never heard of them before—and then I fell madly in love with them.

The magazine was much thinner in those days, so you could read the whole *New Yorker* on the way to work. In the summertime I worked in Manhattan and I lived in the Bronx, so that was an hour on the subway, so I could read the whole thing . . . or there and back. I was a fast reader in those days.

I'm so glad that *The New Yorker* didn't die. The only thing I object to now is that there's too much to read and the articles are too long. I can't keep up, and I hate to throw them out.

First Flash: candy from a Stranger—Porn, Dirty Books, and Obscene Phone calls

CHAPTER 8

Experimental Theater

CATHERINE, BOOKSTORE MANAGER, 23

Partway through my senior year of high school, I'd gotten a job at an artificially French sandwich and espresso café in the mall. Despite the uniforms, it was a fun job, or rather, I liked the nominal cash and it wasn't humiliating and the food was edible. Most of the other employees were my age and had a generic disrespect for the establishment, and we spent after-hours time at Greek diners drinking coffee and smoking cigarettes. I had no boyfriend to talk about, but I liked music and followed politics and we were all from the Virginia suburbs and had mutual friends. We sometimes talked about sex, which is to say, the theory of it, without being theoretical or thoughtful or otherwise enlightening.

One night a few weeks after high school graduation, I was at home doing nothing. Amy from the café called. She was about to finish her shift and was looking for something to do. I grabbed the movie listings from the newspaper and drove to the mall to meet her. Either nothing interesting was playing, or we couldn't decide what to see between blockbusters and subtitles, or we missed some showing or other. "Ha ha," we snickered, "let's go to the Foxchase." Without too much geographic description, the Foxchase theater is a few miles away from the mall; technically a few towns over. It cohabits in a plaza with a Korean-Chinese restaurant and a dinner theater, and it shows second-run foreign and independent films on one screen, and "pornographic" X-rated features on the other. It was no secret. The movie listings were printed right there in the paper.

I'd had an article that I had just read about exotic dancers from *Sassy* magazine stuck in the back of my mind, and I think that had influenced the whole sex-themed evening. And this was the most daring thing I could do, legally. Petty vandalism and faux thuggery weren't my scene, and seeing a porn movie seemed sophisticated and urbanely hip. So we bought the tickets, and we weren't carded. I forget the title, but the movie was in Dutch with English subtitles. There weren't a lot of people in the theater, and we sat in the first few rows, off to the side. Someone was seated behind Amy, somewhat slouched into a fetal position.

The premise of the film was actually rather appealing and, in retrospect, slightly prophetic. A pop singer with pigtails and ribbons who sang songs about lollipops and posed for portraits in pink with teddy bears had a cocaine-fueled flashback to her earlier days. In the studio she started to have a breakdown about a film made before her fame, and the recollection of this memory drove her to hire a private detective to find the reel so it could be destroyed and prevent the undermining of her career. Travel across Europe ensued, with, of course, lots of sex to be had. Hand jobs, a *Kama Sutra*–style multiples scene with a lady guru who did five guys at once with her mystical Eastern ways. There might have been some narration I missed, indicating a dream sequence, and it could truly have been the pop star tapping into something Jungian about the tantric ways of women, but I can't be certain. The sex scenes weren't subtitled. The incriminating film was eventually recovered, potential blackmail averted. The finer points of the movie are lost to me now.

The lights went on, Amy and I stood up, stretched and looked around and saw mostly unaccompanied men. They stared blandly at us, as we stared at them. We rushed off to the ladies' room, and at the sinks we confided to each other that we had been dying to go to the bathroom the whole time but each of us felt mildly alarmed about leaving the other alone. Especially after, Amy noted, the seat behind her started rocking and thrusting with hypnotic regularity.

We went to the Greek diner a few miles away where we analyzed the sex, the hair, the attractiveness of the people, the hilarious Euro-ness of it all, with the fervor of amateur film critics and the jaded air of too-smart-for-our-own-good teenagers. I tried to conceal my woeful lack of experience, although it wasn't really necessary, since the movie offered enough to discuss without getting personal. During the course of drinking our coffee and milkshake at the diner, a man in the next booth peered under the glass partition and said sternly, "Would you girls keep it down? You two are screaming." I think he was on a date.

After about two hours of discussion, I drove Amy home and then attempted to sleep—to no avail. I blamed my insomnia on the fleshy bacchanal that was playing on the projector behind my eyes. It would roll and roll, with disordered vignettes of the various positions and gushings and groans, until, each time, it was interrupted with, "Would you girls keep it down? You are screaming."

I tried to figure out if I was disturbed by the images, and clinically assessed that I wasn't. Overwhelmed, definitely. I was a girl who had been kissed only once and was currently wondering whether the boy I was seeing was ever going to start groping, and if he did, should I push him away just for show? Even if all I wanted was to be groped?

I've only seen one or two other X-rated features since then, again in the name of science, but I don't remember anything about them either, except they were very boring. No adventure, no narrative structure, and no romance.

First Porn

CARLY, ADULT ENTERTAINMENT PUBLICIST, 27

The very first time I saw a nudie picture was on the playground in sixth grade. One of the boys at my school came across a magazine and gleefully shredded it into pieces, then threw the pages into the air, where the wind carried them across the swingsets and jungle gyms like X-rated confetti.

One of the pages landed at my foot. I bent down and picked it up and let my eyes soak in the image of a bottle blonde sitting on the edge of a tub, her hair teased sky high, her frosted blue shadowed eyes closed in ecstasy as her frosted pink lips opened just enough for the tip of her tongue to escape. There were bubbles all over the place. I quickly threw it away, immediately feeling dirty at having absorbed the image and somehow burning it into my memory. Yet at the same time I was titillated, and just a little intrigued.

So I had seen nudie pictures before, but I never dreamed that what I saw in the pictures could be live-action entertainment fodder for your VCR as well—until the day I went into my father's desk. I was in his home office looking for a blue pen so I could do my homework. I looked in his top drawer—nothing. His side drawer? Nothing. Then his bottom drawer . . . and there they were: two blank videotapes that I thought he had hidden to keep me from taping over what was on them with my Madonna music videos.

I popped the first of the two tapes. The tape started in the middle of a scene. They were out in a forest, the wind blowing just slightly, the sun starting to set in the background. Another blonde, this time with a bad perm, knelt in all her naked glory in front of a guy with his pants around his knees and this . . . *thing* was sticking out, and she was putting it in her mouth, licking it, sucking it, smiling and laughing periodically like she liked it. I half-wondered if it was flavored like cherries with the way she was acting.

I sat and watched quietly as he pushed her back into the grass and kissed his way down her torso, pausing to nibble her nipples, then diving between her legs where he licked her "hoo hah," sticking his fingers inside and jerking them around like he was scratching her insides really hard. She must've been itchy because she seemed to like it, but then he stuck his *thing* inside her hole . . . and pulled it out . . . and stuck it in . . . and pulled it out . . . and she laughed and moaned and smiled and moved with him. At the end he sat on her chest, and she squeezed her boobs around his *thing*, and he rubbed against her until he shot white goo all over her. Fearing I'd get caught, I rewound the tape to where it started when I first put it in the VCR, and hid it back in the drawer where I found it.

It took me a few days to fully process what I had seen and how it made me feel. It was shocking to me, but not in a gory way. I knew that they were having sex, but what didn't compute with me was that they were having sex for *fun*. At nine, I had read a book called *Where Did I Come From?* so I knew the basic mechanics of what was happening on that tape I watched. But I had thought you only had sex for making babies, not for fun. What was so fun about making babies? I didn't understand it, nor did I understand why I wanted to see the tape again.

And so I started a torrid affair with that tape, watching that same scene over and over again until I memorized the exact moment that the sun set while they fucked, the bug that landed on the camera lens, the gleeful expression on the girl's face as the guy shot his mighty load between her tits and up her neck. But then shame overcame me. I felt dirty and wrong about watching two people I didn't know having fun with baby-making . . . none of my other friends were doing that, and surely I was sick and perverted for showing an interest in it.

It took me ten years before I watched another porn movie and embraced its entertainment and educational value. And five years after that I started working in the adult industry as a writer and later a publicist, with a roster of clients including some that I used to watch as a curious consumer.

Heading for Fame

CATHY, COPYWRITER, 37

I guess I've been a star-fucker all my life. When I was in first grade, I pretended my life-sized stuffed snowman was Bobby Sherman, and I made out with it constantly. After Bobby came Donny. I sent the exact same letter every single day to Osmond headquarters: Dear Donny, I love you. Love, Cathy.

When I included one of my father's purple-themed ties (to match Donny's ever-present purple socks), my letter-writing campaign finally paid off with a form letter from the Donny Osmond Fan Club and a mimeographed headshot of the Don, rubber-stamped with his little-kid signature. Of course, I had expected

Donny to make a personal appearance at my front door, thanking me profusely for my extravagant and thoughtful gift. So when he chose to send a carbon-copied headshot instead, the love affair was over.

Four years later my eleven-year-old love life was resurrected when Vinnie Barbarino took his seat in Mr. Kotter's classroom. That Breck girl hair . . . those pale sky eyes . . . those painted-on Sergios . . . he was possibly the only guy who could pull off wearing an eight-inch comb in his back pocket. John Travolta's appeal was apparent. He was one big hunk of juvenile delinquency. And for a teacher's pet like me, he was enough to induce some major Carter-brand panty knots.

When Vinnie became Tony, leaving the schoolyard for the dance floor, I was ready to follow suit (white, three-piece, polyester). But *Saturday Night Fever* was rated R, which in the parent code stands for "Rong." My father was concerned with four-letter words and what he called "adult themes." But as it turned out, those issues should have been the least of his worries.

Because despite a topless dancer scene, a knifey gang fight between Tony's crew and the Barracudas, and little Bobby's swan dive off the Verrazano, all I wanted to talk about (when I finally got to see the movie) was what Annette was doing to Tony in the backseat of his car. "Just give me a blowjob," he said. I had no idea why her feathered hair suddenly dipped below camera range, but I did have the vague sense that some kind of sex was going on. And if that Donna Pescow was doing some kind of sex thing to my John, I was going to find out about it.

The next day I cornered my mother in her bedroom.

"Mommy, what's a blowjob?"

I once asked her if she knew how to tie a French knot, and she instead explained the mechanics of a French kiss, so I figured she had some understanding of below-the-belt shenanigans.

"A what?"

"Blowjob. It was what this lady did to John Travolta in the movie."

"Well," she began, "do you know what oral sex is?"

"Yeah. It's when you talk dirty to someone."

"You just keep on thinking that."

That didn't stop me. I knew blowjobs weren't as simple as that. I went downstairs to the den, where my father and David, my nine-year-old brother, were watching golf on the TV.

"Daddy, what's a blowjob? I heard it in the movie last night. Do you know what one is?"

I watched my Dad for any clues. He looked like a cartoon character that just slammed his thumb with a giant hammer—bulging eyes, red face, hyperbolic beads of sweat.

"That's the last time I let one of Mommy's friends take you to the movies."

Now I was on to something. My mom, who normally swore like a sailor, wasn't talking. And I hadn't seen my dad so flustered since David asked him if making love felt like a back scratch.

"*I wanna know what a blowjob is!!!*" Only now, repeating this story with the knowledge of what I was asking, do I feel completely mortified.

My brother, who had watched the whole exchange in silence, was now snickering.

"You're so stupid," he said in that tough little-kid voice that always made me want to punch him. "It's a douche. A tampon."

My father just sat there with this "where did I go wrong" mixed with a "thank God" look on his face.

A few days later I consulted our home reference library: an archived collection of my father's *Playboy* and *Penthouse* magazines. I had usually paged through his dirty magazines in search of funny cartoons. I also devoured the bios of each month's *Playboy* centerfold, especially their turn-ons and turn-offs.

I took a stack of magazines into the bathroom and, concentrating on the Penthouse Forum ("I never thought this would happen to me, but . . ."), finally pieced everything together.

When I had it all figured out, I had one more question for my mother: "Why would any girl want to do this? Even to John Travolta?"

"You'll see," was all she said.

Bedtime Stories

ADRIENNE, REALTOR, 38

The summer that Nixon resigned, I was nine and spending the summer in Norway. My uncle, who was in his late thirties at the time, was living in my grandparents' old apartment in Oslo. I slept in a daybed in this huge living room. There were all these bookshelves in there, teeming with these stupid books with dirty nurse cartoons. On the bottom shelf there were all these magazines, including a big stack of *Playboy* magazines. At night I couldn't sleep, so I pulled out the books and *Playboys* and started looking at them. I spent several weeks that summer at night after everyone had gone to bed, looking at the pictures. The pictures of the women fascinated me. I felt like I wasn't supposed to be looking at them or that the magazines were supposed to be looked at in private, so I was getting access to something that was a little bit forbidden. Not bad or dirty, just private.

I was really interested in what women's bodies looked like. I remember doing a lot of comparing, looking at my body and the bodies of the women in these pictures. I think women look at other women. It's something we do in a way that men don't look at other men. It's something that we do reflexively—we're drawn to look at other women. I don't think it's a question of competition. It's like this sense of sisterhood.

That whole summer was really about sex—reading those dirty nurse cartoons with the lecherous doctors and nurses with enormous breasts bursting out of their little uniforms. I was exposed to the kinds of jokes men make about women, what men fantasize about.

I didn't understand at the time what would make my uncle want to look at those pictures. I'd never been exposed to nudie girls in any conscious way, but on some level I knew that this was something men liked. I think there's a certain aspect of male sexuality that was just very alien to me. I grew up in this very, very female family. Even my uncle was raised by women and doted on by women. So there was this secret little cache of male sexuality in a home that was so female-dominated. And even though it was his home, there were all the ghosts of everyone else. My grandparents were dead, and my uncle lived in their apartment with a female housekeeper.

The pathetic thing is, I was in Norway two years ago, and my uncle still has those same magazines from the early 1970s. He's so cheap he even recycles his porn.

In Living Color

DORI, CHILDCARE ADVOCATE, 26

Me and my best friend were together all the time. Her dad used to drive us everywhere, and I remember one time we were sitting in the backseat, talking about penises. I think we were fifteen. We were discussing what we thought penises looked like. I don't know why, or what we were saying, or what the extent of the conversation was, but it was pretty clear that we didn't know what we were talking about. We also didn't think that her dad was listening.

The very next day I was over at her house, and her dad walked right into her bedroom with a magazine—and it was just wild—it was *Playgirl*, with all these naked men! He gave it to us, and he was like, "If you tell your mothers I'll kill you! This is totally secret."

So we opened the magazine, and the first picture we saw was of this man . . . naked . . . a white guy. Just totally naked. No clothes, no costumes. When you think penis, you kind of think about when you wiped your little baby cousin's while changing his diaper. You forget that there are testicles. And I think that was the strangest part. What is that just hanging there?!

That was the first time we saw a penis, and we had no idea what it looked like or what it was supposed to be. It wasn't what we imagined at all.

After we saw the penis, all conversation was over. We put the magazine away and were grossed out and never wanted to see it again. But we were very surprised her dad did something like that. I think that that was a turning point, knowing: Oh my God! (a) he thinks we're old enough to see naked men, and (b) he is acknowledging the fact that we were curious. And I think that we respected that very much. But it was still really, really strange.

Romance Writer
SARA, LAW STUDENT, 24

I had always seen *Playboy* magazines and was fascinated by them. Then I found out there was *Playgirl*, with naked men, and I was like, "I have to get my paws on one of those!" At the time I think I was about ten or eleven, and my brother was fourteen or fifteen. He had been drinking for a long time; he was like the wild child. I saw him at a drugstore and he had been drinking and he said, "What the hell, I'll buy it for you!"

I had that *Playgirl* for probably three years—the same one! I thought it was kind of gross, but I remember also thinking it was exciting and scandalous: "Oh my goodness, here's a naked man!" I don't know if I'd ever seen a naked man before.

My favorite part was the erotic stories. My best friend and I were obsessed with them. We'd read them again and again, and we wanted to write our own—but we didn't understand all the "terminology." We started to write this story; I think it was the fourth or fifth grade. It was about the kids in our class who we thought had crushes on each other. One part was about a student and a teacher. We'd read the *Playgirl* stories and tried to put those words and phrases into our story, even though we didn't really know what they meant—we just knew it was sex. I remember one line we thought sounded really sexual: "He went down to explore the horizon." But we weren't sure what *horizon* meant.

At the time we had a housekeeper who would also drive me to extracurricular activities. My friend and I had been working on this story for about a month or so. It was a real work in progress. So the housekeeper was driving us somewhere, and I was like, "What does horizon mean?" I knew it did have a real meaning, but I didn't necessarily know if it could also be used to mean something dirty.

She defined it as "the sky meets the land." And we were like, "Okay, that doesn't work!"

Apparently we had the story with us in the car. Well, I left a couple pages of the story in the car, and a little while later the housekeeper came and took me aside. She was a Jehovah's Witness, and she was cleaning out her car before driving some of the top Jehovah's Witness honchos to a meeting, and she found the pages of the story. It was really a dirty story! We were using every word we could find from the *Playgirl* stories in our story. She couldn't understand what the story was about or where it came from, until she saw the word *horizon* and she put it all together and realized it was us!

She was livid. "What if the Jehovah's Witnesses found it and read it? What would they have thought of me?" And I asked, "Well, where is my story?" She had thrown it away, and I was so upset, because we had put so much work into that story, and we loved it so much and it was all gone!

I held on to that *Playgirl* for years. I hid it under all these other papers and magazines in my white filing cabinet drawer under my desk. I don't know what happened to it. I think I hit a point where I felt I shouldn't have it. Not that I felt dirty about having it, but I did feel guilty. And after three years, I thought, "I'm older now, I'm mature, and I don't need this anymore." But I wish I still had that story I wrote!

Miss Dialed
AMBER, IMPROV COMEDIENNE, 27

This happened when I wasn't too young, but I also wasn't old enough to actually understand what was unfolding. So I was probably eight years old. My parents had gone out for the night, and I was home with my brother, who's five years older than me. He stayed home a lot to look after me when we were little.

My brother and I were sitting in the living room watching TV and it was pretty early in the evening, maybe eight o'clock. I remember everything exactly about it: we were sitting by the coffee table, and the light on the ceiling fan was halfway on and halfway off. The phone rang, and we had one of those prototypes of a cordless phone that was really heavy with the long metal antenna. I lunged toward the phone to pick it up because I guess children sometimes want to pick up the phone when the parents are gone so they feel like an adult—I guess that's what was going through my head. My brother didn't want me to pick it up, and he kept trying to get the phone away from me, and I kept shooing him away.

A man was on the other end of the line, and he asked me if I was home alone, if my parents were there. I didn't tell him that my parents weren't there, because I wasn't *that* dumb. But I stayed on the phone with him, and he kept talking, and I was listening as my brother kept trying to get the phone away from me. He was asking, "Who is it? Who is it?" But I didn't want to concede to my brother, to give him the phone and say, "Yes, you're the adult," because, of course, I was an independent little brat.

So I stayed on the phone, and this man was asking questions about my mom. He was asking, "Do you get in the shower with your mom?" I don't think that I was answering any questions, but he just kept asking. I didn't understand that what he was saying was bad; I didn't know what he was getting at, because I was not old enough to understand it. But I knew that it was wrong, and I could feel it.

Then he started asking me questions like "Does your mommy have hair between her legs?" And "Does your mommy wash you while you're in the shower?" That's when I realized that this really wasn't right. I don't remember if he said anything else after that, because I probably repressed the rest. I hung up the phone, and my brother kept asking who it was, and I wouldn't tell him what happened. I went off to be by myself.

For the next few weeks after that, I cried myself to sleep. I couldn't tell my mom that it happened. I don't know why; it's not like I knew what he was getting at, but I just knew it was bad, dirty, and wrong, and that I shouldn't say anything about it.

I think I felt like I was somehow responsible for the whole episode. Especially because my brother tried to take the phone away from me and I wouldn't let him. If I'd just given him the phone, it wouldn't have happened. So I kind of felt it was my fault.

I also felt really bad because my family is really open about stuff, and this call was something that, for whatever reason, I couldn't talk to them about. So it felt like a secret, and that felt bad.

I thought about this phone call for a long time. I thought about it a lot until my early teen years. I was traumatized by it. And only very recently did I tell my mother about it. Through high school and college I forgot about it; I didn't think about it anymore, it just kind of was gone. But all those feelings came out again when I told the story to a friend of mine. I was shocked that I'd even remembered it.

I decided that I wanted to finally tell my mom. We recently went on a bonding-type trip to Arizona, and the first night we were there I started to tell her about it. My heart was racing, and I was getting choked up. Telling her was really strange—I felt like that little kid again. And I'm telling her about something that really, really upset me. I said, "I don't know if I've ever told you this story, but I'm going to tell you, and if I have told you, then tell me I have, because I don't remember telling you. And if I haven't, then this may seem strange, but I feel like I should tell you, because this is something that I've pressed down for a long time."

When I got to the part about him asking if she had hair between her legs, she burst out laughing. She thought that was really funny. She asked what he sounded like and did I feel like I knew him. Then she said, "Wait a minute, don't even answer that."

After I told her, I somehow thought I would feel this great weight lift. And as I was telling her about it, my eyes kept welling up, like I would cry. It wasn't that I felt upset; it was that I almost felt really excited that I was getting the whole memory out, like the tears were washing it out.

First Fallacy: Lies, All Lies

CHAPTER 9

White(bread) Lie

SARAH, ATTORNEY, 26

It happened when I was in the middle of a conversation with friends of mine, eating lunch in the Wesleyan college cafeteria. In the middle of the conversation I realized that this impression I'd been laboring under all my life was not true. I realized suddenly, in the middle of this conversation with friends, that it wasn't true that all the vitamins rose to the crust of the bread.

I don't remember the first time my mother told me this; I must have been five. I always accepted this as true: that in the baking process—the reason you had to eat the crust—was because the vitamins would kind of expand to the edges. And I guess I did wonder about how they extended to the edges and not just up to the top. And so in the middle of this conversation with all my friends, I realized that this was not true.

It was this sudden Dawn-Breaks-Over-Marblehead awakening moment: "Oh my God! It's not true!" I'm like eighteen years old, and I thought all along that vitamins in the bread were all in the crust.

I guess there was an element of "What else? What else did my mother tell me? What else isn't true?" But strangely enough, I don't think that this realization made me revise any of the other stuff she told me. Because my mom says a lot of really wacky things. When you just come up with something that's completely untrue, there's a joke for it in my family: it's called the hair dye theory.

The hair dye theory is a story that my mom told her sisters, about a phenomenon that happens when you dye your hair: some complete, long, garbled argument about how the hair dye drips off the ends of your hair, and that's why you get dark roots, rather than because your hair simply grows out.

At any rate there was never really any reason for me to believe my mother—and when I realized this . . . it was very embarrassing to realize this in public in front of all my friends, and to do so very visibly. "The crusts aren't where all the vitamins are!" And my friends are like, "Uh, yeah. That's what you've been thinking all this time?" And I'm like, "Uh-huh, yeah, it made sense!" At that point I wasn't any more suspicious of my mother. I didn't feel that she was all that trustworthy to begin with. This just made me feel like, "Oh my God! I believed this junk!"

Striking Out

SUE, CHEF, 26

I remember the first time I lied to my father, because it was also the first time I "got the belt." I was in the fourth grade, and I was nine years old and living with my family on a military base in northern Germany. Near our house there was a small park, just some swings and a slide and a little bit of open green space. There was also a little utility shed with a lawn mower and a little can of gas.

I tended to play with two boys in particular, John and Allen. That day in the park one of us had gotten a book of matches, I don't remember who, but having them made us want to start a little fire. So we started gathering sticks and little pieces of grass. It was an overcast day and a little bit misty, so we decided it would be better to have our fire in the shed. Plus, I think that we wanted our activities to be kept as secret as possible. So we made our little pile and huddled around. And there was this one little kid named David who was also there, and David was protesting. He was not happy about what we were doing; he thought it was wrong and that we were bad. He was probably about six.

I lit the fire. We all knew how to light matches, but I just think the other kids were scared and were afraid they'd get in trouble. I guess I just didn't understand the severity of what we were doing. The lawn mower was right next to the little fire, there was a gas can, and the lawn mower was full of gas. So there was a danger, we just weren't aware of it. So as we were doing this, David ran home, and the next thing we knew, his dad came. He was the commanding officer of the base and therefore the most elite person. So when David ran to tell his dad, and his dad came, we were further humiliated by knowing that there could be some repercussions for our parents, because an officer had found the lowly enlisted men's children starting fires in the park.

I remember his dad had a cheesy little mustache. He yelled, "What are you doing?!" He stamped out our little fire and told us all to go home. Then he came around to each of our houses to talk to our parents.

By then my dad had talked to some of the other kids' parents, and someone told that I lit the fire, that I was the one who struck the match. So my father asked me, "Did you do that?" And I said, "No. Allen did it."

I don't know if he smelled foul play or if he could somehow tell that I was lying, but I was scared. Probably both, since most likely Allen and John corroborated the match-lighting story. My dad continued asking me about the matches, having me recount the story, and interrogating me until I cracked. And when I cracked, he took me up to my room and just bent me over his knee and took his belt out—the belt that he used to double up and snap to put the fear into my sisters and me when we were misbehaving. But we were never hit; I think that each of us "got the belt" maybe once in our lives. So the whole cracking of the belt was my father practicing intimidation and threats.

But he really carried through this time and gave me a good whacking.

The worst part of being punished by my dad was what preceded the belt. Because what preceded any physical punishment was the lecture: "Look at me when I'm talking to you!" So you're sort of bewildered and fearful and you have to look at the person, this big man with the beard and mustache, who you know is your disciplinarian.

This time there was definitely the lecture before the belt: "Lying is really awful, it's most important in your life to be honest and not lie, it's the most important virtue." This is what he always told me, and this was the incident that really drove it home for me. I guess I stayed up in my room for a while afterward, probably nursing my wounds. It's pretty bewildering to be hit. It kind of takes the punishment to another level and makes you feel pretty shitty about yourself. I probably just sat up there feeling sorry for myself.

When I finally came downstairs, my dad had me come up on his lap, and he said he was sorry. That was kind of freaky too, that whole let's-make-up thing . . . you know, "It hurts me more than it hurts you." Whatever! He didn't say that, thank goodness, but that was the gist of it. He told me that he loved me and he only did that because he was upset that I had lied, and what we did was really bad, yada, yada, yada. Then he told me that we were going to go to the circus the following week.

Cooked-up Story
BONNIE, CHIROPRACTOR, 53

I was in high school. One of the major streets in this upstate city in New York in the early 1960s was sort of a dividing line between families that were more working class and the white-collar professional community.

In my teenage mind I thought that the Jewish families who were Holocaust survivors were poor because they had an accent and lived on the other side of the street. One of my classmates was from one of those families. So I thought I would help her family out. (Mind you, I came from a middle-class family. But I thought we were wealthy compared to my girlfriend, whose family was from Hungary and were survivors.)

My mother was a great cook. She had a freezer in our finished basement where she would store meat she bought on sale and to use for future cooking. So I went down to the basement quietly and stole the meat out of the freezer and walked through the neighborhood to the main street. I crossed it and very quietly walked up to my friend's house and left the frozen meat by the front door. I hid in a prickle bush until my girlfriend's mother opened the front door and found this thawed-out wrapped-up meat and said to her daughter in her thick Hungarian accent, "Bibi, what is this meat doing here? I do not understand who is leaving this meat at our front door."

Bibi, my friend, looked at her mother and said, "I have no idea what you are talking about."

In the meantime my mother, who was very organized, had a list of all that was in her freezer. When she used something, she would cross it off her list. She would go into the freezer looking for chicken or meat to cook a meal and would find that it was missing. After several times noticing this and feeling very puzzled about why this meat was missing, she started to accuse our cleaning lady—a wonderful, caring, dear woman who had been with our family for many years. I could not bear the thought that my mother was blaming innocent, sweet Juanita, who had nothing to do with the missing meat.

So I 'fessed up. My loving mother, who wanted to chastise me, knew that what I was doing was out of love. She embraced me instead. It was a very tender moment of youth at its best.

Arrested Development
CLAIRE, RESTAURANT MANAGER, 32

Once upon a time I was a third grader who was completely in love with the most popular boy in her class, the exotic, almond-eyed prince named Jason. The rest of the girls in the class were also deeply in love with him, so I spent from September to December loving him from a distance. Over the Christmas school break I remember praying every night, "Please, God. Please let Jason love me, too." I don't think I had even said one word to Jason at that stage of the game. I was mostly always on the outskirts of things, more the observer than the participator. But in that ever-hopeful time that is third grade, I still believed I had a chance with Jason. And God was going to toss me a bone.

Miraculously, I got back from our Christmas vacation, and lo and behold, our desk assignments had changed. And who was my new tablemate? That's right! There, printed in neat black marker on a crisply folded placard that was placed right next to my crisply folded placard, was the answer to my prayers: Jason S. My mother used to joke that her mother, my grandmother, had a direct line to God—and I truly believed that now I had one, too.

So I naturally worked my magic, and by the end of three days Jason was my official boyfriend, holding my hand under the desk, pushing his tray behind mine in the cafeteria, eating his after-school snacks at my house a few times a week. And the deep-rooted sense that I always had, that Jason would like me, really like me, if only he got to know me, was made real.

One day after we had been playing together (because that's really what dating was back then), Jason asked if I could sleep over at his house over the weekend. It sounded like a reasonable request, since I often had my friends stay over on weekends. So I told him I'd ask my mom and get back to him the next day at school.

So I asked her. "Mommy, can I sleep over at Jason's house this weekend?"

And she said, "No, you cannot."

"But why?"

And these were the words that would become etched in my memory: "Because it's illegal for boys and girls to sleep in the same room unless they're married."

Which sounded like a perfectly logical explanation to me. My mother was raising me on old 1940s musicals, and anytime a "couple" tried to register at a hotel, they always had to be married (or at least register as Mr. and Mrs.).

The next day at school, while on line at the cafeteria, I sadly explained the law to Jason. He thought about it a moment and then looked at me very seriously. And again, another set of words that would become etched in my memory: "Claire," he began, "I like you, I like you, I like you, I like you, I like you." After about three minutes of "I like you's," Jason said, "One more like would be a love. But I love Renee." Renee just happened to be a new girl in school, who I thought looked just like Snow White.

Fast-forward about ten years, to freshman year in college. My boyfriend and I wanted to go into New York City to see our favorite band, Squeeze. The problem was, getting back to New Jersey after the show would mean missing the last bus home. "So what?" said my boyfriend. "We'll just get a cheap hotel room and leave the next morning."

I was horrified. "We can't do that!"

"Why not? I have the money to pay."

"It's illegal."

"What!?" he said.

"It's illegal to get a hotel room together because we're not married."

"Did your mother tell you that?" was all he said.

So I called my mother pretty soon after that embarrassing little interlude. I told her, "You were always trying to ruin my good time!"

And you know what she said? "I had heard Jason was a very fast boy. I was trying to protect you."

Maybe that was at the center of a lot of the lies my mother told me. (Yes, there were more to come.) She knew the truth would be harder for me to take or, in third grade, completely impossible to understand. But as I saw it, my short romance with the most popular boy in class was the end of the road for me. Jason was my "captain of the football team, prom king, tall, dark, and handsome." I felt like I never had that it-girl moment again.

First Flicker: Recognizing the Power of T&A

CHAPTER 10

Secret Weapon

KYM, PROJECT MANAGER, 46

I was all of seven and such a tomboy. I always hung out with my two brothers and the boys who lived next door. There were six of us: Scott, Daryl, Craig, Greggy, Joe, and me. It didn't matter that I was the only girl; I did whatever the boys did, including fighting. There was this one kid in the neighborhood that everyone hated. His name was Butch, and he was the biggest bully. He even had a really mean dog, a huge German shepherd named Conga who used to chase all the kids around the neighborhood. So the dog just added fuel to the fire as to why we didn't like this guy.

One day Butch got himself a new pair of tennis shoes. Now, this was the 1960s, so they were probably PF Flyers. And they were *white*; I mean WHITE. It's true, whenever you got new tennis shoes, everyone at school tried to break them in for you by stepping all over them and leaving a mark. So we had this dastardly plan for how we were going to mess up Butch's sneakers.

We decided to dig a mud pit in our backyard. It was about a foot deep, filled with mud, and covered with grass and leaves. We tried to make it like quicksand, so Butch would sink real fast. We got the idea from Tarzan, because he always had quicksand in his movies.

When we finished building the pit, it was time to get Butch to come on over and play—and I was the lure. I was supposed to stand just behind the mud pit and yell, "Hey, Butch. Want some lemonade? Come on over and stand next to me!"

And Butch came running! He stepped right in front of me and he started sinking, and his new shoes were ruined. He was so mad! He chased us for blocks. We were laughing so hard that we had trouble outrunning the kid.

That day I experienced power. I had no tits, no ass, but I was a woman. I learned the power of being that female lure, that CIA babe with a come-hither mission, the allure of a woman promising a man some treats. Even my brothers knew the plan would work. When I said I couldn't believe that Butch fell for it, they said, "Men will do anything for a woman."

Here Kitty, Kitty

JANE, PERFORMANCE ARTIST, AGE IS A SECRET

There was this Tootsie Roll commercial, "How many licks does it take to get to the center of a Tootsie Roll Pop" and I remember being twelve years old at church camp and having these boys ask me to lick one—and me doing so innocently, not realizing what they were really interested in. They were all getting little hard-ons, watching me!

In my mind, I did realize that I was doing something sexual. I didn't know what a hard-on was; I knew the slang, but not the actual mechanics of it until later in high school. But I did know about sexual arousal, I'd seen movies, I knew when guys were interested, and when a woman was doing something sexy or seductive. I didn't start out that way, but as I was doing it, I remember feeling, "I have power right now. I have power over them." It was this sexual power that you feel as a virgin that I don't think you can ever truly feel again. Maybe when you're a woman and you're still young and thin and a guy really wants you, maybe you can still have that power, but I don't think anything is as powerful as having your virginity as a wanted item, you know?

It was interesting because at the time I was dating the preacher's son. We dated from twelve to fifteen. We only kissed. We went a whole year doing nothing, then the second year we held hands, and the third year we kissed. We were very good and very pure.

The catcalls began around the same age, at twelve. The things that made me feel I was turning into someone different were always things that made me feel like I had power, whether it was personal power, spiritual power, or some sense of enlightenment. That's why I love the story of Socrates. I first heard about him in the third grade. I felt that that was a moment of truth and that was how I felt about the world as well. It was a moment of insight, that "I am different from these other people." I knew I had substance and courage and was brave.

I never felt that I was a pretty person or a hot chick, but then walking down the hall and hearing this first catcall and looking around to see where it had come from, and thinking, "Who are they whistling at?" I would never presume that it would be me. I think that was the first year too that I started getting curves and filling out. When I realized that it was for me, I think I might have been scared, thinking, "What does this mean? Are they now labeling and defining me as a person who gets attention for their sexuality, and do I have to become that person now?"

There were always the girls at school who were prettier and used makeup and wore tight clothes, and because they got recognition for that, I think they tried to live up to that expectation. That was a niche that other people were creating for them, and they wanted to live up to it. But I didn't want my niche in life to be something other people created for me. So that school year I made a conscious choice that I didn't want to go that route. It was okay if they thought that of me—it made me feel confident, and it made me feel accepted. But I took that feeling of confidence and acceptance and instead of using it to perpetuate some sense of sexuality that they were seeing, I chose instead to run for school president.

Last Dance

MEGAN, RECEPTIONIST, 24

I was a bridesmaid in my cousin's wedding when I was twelve. The guy she married was wonderful—he still is—and he had a bunch of brothers who were all going to be his groomsmen. The day before the wedding, during the rehearsal, I got paired up with this one brother, who looked a little bit scraggly and weird. I think he was thirtyish. Immediately, when we were walking down the aisle together, he was holding my arm and he whispered in my ear how beautiful he thought I was. When we took a break and were listening to instructions from the priest, he whispered in my ear again, "Hey baby, how old are you?" And I turned back and said, "I'm twelve!" I just didn't know what he wanted, really.

The night went on, and we had fun, and I think he might have gotten drunk. The next day I didn't see him again until the wedding. I think he was deliberately making himself scarce, because I kept hearing one of his other brothers laughing at him and going, "Leave her alone; she's twelve."

The night of the wedding he acted just fine at the actual ceremony, but then we got to the reception, and immediately he was pounding beer, liquor, whatever. We got to the first dance, and all the wedding party members came to dance. I was dancing with him, I don't remember the song, but I remember it just started happening once again, with the little whispers in my ear. "You look beautiful," he kept saying, "I can't believe you're only twelve." Maybe at most I looked fifteen, but I just had this awkward look about me in my opinion. My teeth were totally crooked, my face just looked more babyish than the sharp features that happen in an older look. I think the things that make you look older, like your eyebrows being more defined, I had none of that. I was completely skinny, scrawny, and flat-chested.

The top of my bridesmaid dress was made out of black taffeta, and the back was this big, open diamond cut-out. The skirt was a huge white tutu thing. I liked the dress and thought it was pretty. Plus, it was my first time wearing high heels, so I felt pretty sophisticated—for me. We were dancing, and he had his hand resting in that diamond-shaped hole in the back of my dress, and he kept on with the "I can't believe you're twelve," thing. But then he just sort of dropped the whole age thing and just started kissing my neck, while we were dancing. I remember being a little put off, but kind of giggling about it. It didn't strike me that what he was doing was really nasty, it just struck me as a little bit funny that he was drunk. Then it kind of got annoying, because his kisses were a little bit more slobbering at that point, and wet all over my neck, and I must have looked a little disgusted or horrified by it.

I remember making eye contact with my family, who were sitting at the table with my grandparents. And you know how you dance and spin around? I remember the first time spinning around my family, when he was just whispering in my ear. Then we spin around again, and he's kissing my neck, and then we spin around again, he's still kissing my neck. I see my family and can see my grandpa just looking over a little more intensely, and we spin around one more time, at which point he's just slobbering everywhere, and that's when my grandpa stands up, walks over, taps him, and says, "Excuse me, that's my granddaughter." My grandpa makes him leave and finishes dancing with me. My grandpa says, "Don't dance with him anymore."

I just say, "Thank you." At first it was funny, and I felt flattered that this man thought I was cute and attractive—"You have beautiful eyes, you have beautiful hair," and I thought my hair was just awful. But then when it got to that slobbering neck kiss . . . that was nasty. I just did not like that at all. I could smell the liquor on his breath. And he also was not a good-looking guy. It would have been different if he were a thirty-year-old knight in shining armor. But he had long scraggly hair, a little bit of a scraggly beard growing in, kind of a mountaineer look to him. So I was grateful when my grandpa cut in.

Heaps of Trouble
LENAE, MEDIA PLANNER, 47

I started developing at age nine, and that was when all the attention started. People couldn't believe I was starting to get busty at that age. But the menfolk couldn't make too obvious observations about it because I was still nine years old. But when I turned twelve, oh my God! I knew I had the power because men would constantly look at me and go, "Oooh, dag!"

I remember this guy in the sixth grade. My boobs were already out. That day in elementary school a funeral of the fire marshal was passing by the school, so all the kids were at the window. And this one boy was trying to be slick and trying to get himself a feel. It was the first time I had anyone touch me. It wasn't like he was groping me, but he had his arms crossed, and his hands were touching the sides of my breasts. He was moving his hands just a little bit to try to get the feel of how it felt. I knew what he was doing, but I was pretending I wasn't aware, you know, and thought, "That kind of feels nice."

I took advantage of the boys' attention when I could. And I could tell the girls wanted to do the opposite for me just because they were always jealous. The boys were always trying to come over to my house. But I couldn't have company; my grandmother wasn't having that. I grew up in Northeast Washington, D.C., where I lived in this sort of bubble world. My grandparents wanted to keep me hidden.

I was voted the second sexiest girl in the whole school. This one girl named India Brown—she was fine honey, that girl. She beat me out. But we were the two sexiest women in that whole school. At the time I just didn't have any scruples. She was my friend and everything, but I liked her boyfriend, and I knew he was attracted to me. If there was someone appealing to me, I knew I had the power to take him.

A Lesson in Morality

BONNIE, LAWYER, 26

I didn't even know he was alive until I was a senior in college. I was twenty-one, a philosophy major, and he was my ethics professor. He was thirty-four, and for me, that was huge. Everything really started when I got my midterm back and I was two points away from an A minus. I thought, "I'm going to go argue this, because I want my grade." I called to make an appointment, and he said, "Meet me at Starbucks because I don't like to have office hours in my office."

I met him for coffee, and it was very professional, very professor-student. He asked me to argue why I thought I deserved this A minus. I don't know if my arguments were any good or not because he didn't say anything like, "That makes perfect sense; you're absolutely right."

What he said was, "Would it make you happy to get the two points?"

And I said, "As a matter of fact, it would make me happy."

And he said, "Okay, great. Here are your two points."

I thought that was it, so I started getting my stuff together. And he said, "Wait a minute, what's your story? Where are you from?" And I thought he was just trying to be nice. I started telling him about myself. He was really easy to talk to, and he seemed to care about who I was and what was going on with me.

And then I asked him about himself, and that part was kind of strange, because I never thought of professors as people. We talked for about an hour and had a really nice conversation. And then he said, "Hey, do you want to go get a drink? Let me take you to the bar next door, and let's have some fun."

So we went, and he ended up having like three or four or five beers. I had maybe a third of a glass of wine. Then he said, "I have to go teach a class now." This guy was so unbelievable! Not only did he teach at my school, he taught night classes at several other schools in the area. Then he said, "Hey, after I teach this class, do you want to go shoot some pool?"

I couldn't believe it, but he then left to go teach his class. He didn't seem drunk to me. We met later at this pool hall that was in my neighborhood, and we shot some pool and had a really nice time. He walked me to my dorm and said, "If you ever want to do it again, you know where to find me."

It was kind of strange to me the way the whole affair ended up happening. I didn't think anything about it the first time we went out. He never complimented me on how I looked, he didn't ask for my number, we just talked and had a lot of fun. About a week later I called him up and asked if he wanted to shoot pool again.

I felt excited about seeing him again because I did think he was really handsome. He was about five foot eleven, Italian, olive-colored skin, green eyes, black hair, dressed really well, lots of energy. But I just didn't expect anything to happen. I just thought we were going to play some pool again. That's as far as my thoughts were going. There wasn't any thought like, "Maybe if I'm friends with him, I'll get a better grade." I knew I was going to get a good grade because I was doing well in that class anyway.

I didn't hear from him for a couple days, so I went to stay with friends in New Jersey, because that's where I used to go when I had a lot of studying to do. I was there for a half an hour and I checked my messages. There was one from him saying, "Do you want to go out tonight?" I had barely even unpacked my bags when I turned around and went back to the city. We ate dinner at this new French place downtown. I knew he didn't make a lot of money, because he was not tenured, and I thought there was no reason to go to this expensive dinner since we were just going to be buddies and shoot some pool. But the thought of going to dinner and playing pool with my ethics professor kind of tanta-lized me. "This doesn't happen every day," I thought, "so I have to take this opportunity."

I don't remember what I wore, but whatever it was, I was happy with it. I have really large breasts, so if I don't wear something that is form fitting, I look like a barn. So I'm sure I wore a turtle-neck, jeans, and boots. I met him at this hip new place, and he looked wonderful, and I thought, "Gosh, he looks really nice to be shooting pool." Even though we had reservations, we waited at this teeny-tiny table for an hour before we were seated. We were smooshed up against each other. I was literally so close, I had to lean backward and away from him just to talk. I thought, "This is so inappropriate." We finally got to our table, which was a corner booth, so we sat next to each other. And that was awkward too. The conversation turned to the Unabomber. And I was saying, "People from Montana are so weird. I went to Montana once, and it was horrible. I'd never go back there again. But I actually had my first kiss in Montana, when I was thirteen and on a trip with my parents."

He said, "Tell me about the kiss, I have to hear it!" And when I finished, he pulled me to him and kissed me.

I thought, "Well, now I know what to expect," and just went with the flow. At that point he had downed at least three drinks. He was a serious drinker. The more alcohol that got into him, the bolder he felt. We ended up making out in this booth. The whole rest of dinner, we're talking and kissing and he's drinking and drinking and drinking. We closed the restaurant down. We must have been there about three hours. When we finally left, I asked him what he wanted to do next, and he said, "I am going to take you back to my apartment and make love to you all night." And I was thinking, "Okay, I guess we're not shooting pool."

When we got back to his place, he warned me before taking his shirt off, "I am probably the hairiest person you will ever see." Since he was drunk and since it was our first time, I figured he was just self-conscious and was exaggerating. You would never guess anything by looking at him. I took his sweater off and remember thinking to myself for a split second, "I don't know if I can do this." I'm talking carpet. Then I blurted out, "My God, you look like you still have your sweater on." And then for another split second, I was mortified that I had just said that to my ethics professor, which was strange enough, but of all times to say it right before I was about to sleep with him, which was that much stranger. But he laughed, and I think he thought I had balls for saying that. I'm telling you, if the situation wasn't so naughty and if his face wasn't so handsome and if he wasn't so charming, I would have walked out right then and there. I tried to think of him as a stuffed animal (which I like) and concentrated on that face and those wonderful green eyes.

I spent the night with him, and he was awesome and it was great, and I went home in the morning and I thought, "Oh jeez, what did I do?" Not in a regretful way at all, because I was really happy with the whole experience, but I was still in his class, and we still had a month of school left. And I didn't want him to think I'd planned it or seduced him because of my grade. I think there was this unspoken understanding. We never did talk about it the next morning. He never said, "Don't tell anyone about this. I could lose my job." We both had a wonderful time with one another, and that was how we left it. I figured that even though I had never done anything like this before but he probably had, I would just take his lead. If he wanted to call, he could, and if he wanted to keep his distance, I would understand. And neither one of us called the other. So I didn't speak to him for a month. I took my final, and then I went home to L.A. for my winter break.

The week I got back for spring semester, the second I got back,

I called him. We dated the whole semester. It was a total adventure. He was a really crazy bold guy, and he'd dance with all my friends and twirl them around. He was always so drunk! Vodka gimlets all night long. I remember one time we went out and he left ninety exams at a club. He checked his briefcase at the coat stand, and he got really drunk and was dancing and dancing. We were on the way home when he realized it.

I was at the age where I wanted to test myself out and see who I could get. I knew that there were all these other girls who wanted him, and I got him. And I didn't even set out to get him. I think that's part of why the whole relationship worked so well: it was really organic, and we just let it flow, and if we felt like seeing each other we did, and if we didn't, we didn't. We didn't have to have these big long deep talks. I would go on a date with him and sleep over, and in the morning we would lie in bed and talk about carpentry. One would figure that we would talk about philosophy a lot, but actually we never did, not once. I would make him tell me all about the things he had built and teach me all the technical terms and what the tools were for. Sometimes we even watched *This Old House* together.

We stopped seeing each other maybe a month before school was over. It wasn't intentional. We just kind of drifted apart, the calls became more infrequent. It was fine. I recently did a Google search on him and was surprised to learn that he's still a professor at my school. I think he probably shouldn't be teaching ethics.

Branching Out

I wear the watch that my maternal grandfather wore every day of his life until his eyes got too cloudy to tell time. On the back of the watch is an inscription: Joe Kane Architect of our dreams. My grandfather had designed a home for a well-to-do couple, and in gratitude they gifted

him with the solid gold Patek Philippe watch. I always thought their dedication read like it should be on a tombstone.

My grandfather died June 4, 1993. He gave me the watch years before he died. I guess he wanted to see me enjoy it, the feel of the heavy gold

against my thin wrist, the weight of it all. It's the only thing I ever wanted of my grandfather's— because it had his name on it.

The night before his funeral, my mother asked me if I needed a sleeping pill. She misread my blank face and steady eyes as indicators of an

FIRST FRATERNITY:
BREAKING INTO THE
BOYS' CLUB

p. 166

overwrought mind. I knew that the situation required me to exhibit the proper emotional distress, but the truth is, I couldn't muster it.

"How come I've cried harder and longer over breakups with stupid boyfriends," I asked my mother, "when I should be crying the most for Poppy?"

I realize now that I was wrestling with one of the greatest philosophical questions of all time. By experiencing my first "important" death (as well as being offered a sleeping pill—a true badge of adulthood), my unexplored universe was getting

larger and larger. I was going from a visceral plane (filled with boys and beds and every variation of the five senses) to someplace way more cerebral.

Welcome to the real world. After the wish fulfillment (the joyful and powerful emblems of womanhood and the privileges that go along with it) comes the

winter of our discontent. Yes, it's the big ol' slap of life—or death, as some of the stories in this section prove.

To truly grow is to suffer setbacks: a rotten job, a bout of depression, a loss of a friend. Because without knowing

vulnerability and fragility, how do we express gratitude and appreciation? Setbacks in life are the metal slugs that keep the scale in balance. They're what keep you soft and mushy. And they're also what make you tough.

First Fraternity: Breaking into the Boys' club

CHAPTER 11

Drum Solo

KOPANA, FILM PRESERVATIONIST, 37

I've always played drums. I can't think of a time when I've not played drums. I taught myself. My mother's side of the family was pretty musical. Her dad played guitar and banjo. Mom can strum a little bit; she played piano in church, and she'd actually played marching drums in the high school band. She didn't teach me though. My dad can't carry a tune in a bucket. He's so totally tone deaf. He can't even pat his foot in time.

But I have just always played. I clearly remember finally being tall enough to reach into the drawer and get out butter knives. I destroyed tons of my mother's furniture. And so one of the things my grandmother did to try to save whatever furniture we had left was to save her lard buckets—her one-, three-, and five-pound lard buckets. They made great drums. So I would play the buckets with knives, spoons, or whatever. And then when I was four years old, my mother gave me a tambourine. I still have it. And that was all fine and well, but it wasn't a drum. When I was six, she got me some bongos. I've still got those, too. But those weren't drums either. So when I was eight, she finally bought me a snare drum. But that still wasn't a whole drum set. I had to work her into what it was I was really after.

I remember one Christmas my parents got me one of those paper drum sets from JC Penney, and it lasted about fifteen minutes. The next year they tried it again, and it lasted about as long. When I was ten, we moved to Arizona because my mother had really bad allergies and her doctor advised us to up and move from Kentucky to the desert. So we did. And when we moved to Arizona, my mother went into an antiques store and found a five-piece set of drums for $110. So that was my first drum set. I got them when I was ten and played on them until I was fourteen, when we moved back home to West Liberty, Kentucky, and I sold them.

When I got back here, my grandmother really, really, really wanted me to come play at the Pentecostal church, because, you know, they had this little choir, and there were people who could play guitar and whatnot, but they really needed a drummer. So my grandmother bought me—little did I know at the time—a 1968 set of Ludwigs from a guy there in West Liberty. He had the set in his basement, wasn't playing them. Bought them for $250. A five-piece set. And I've still got those. I got those when I was fourteen. I made my first recordings on those.

And that's what I was doing. I was playing in church on Sundays, and then I'd go play country and rock and roll around town with some of my schoolteachers. The guy who taught art used to dress like Waylon Jennings, and I ended up taking four years of art because I could smoke in his class.

So the teachers and I were having a little jam session at somebody's garage, and this guy named Linville comes by. I'd known Linville my whole life. Everybody in West Liberty knows Linville. For whatever reason, West Liberty started this festival called the Sorghum Festival. After a few years, somehow Linville came to be in charge of the entertainment, and he always seemed to invite the same bands over and over and over and over again.

So anyway, here I was jamming in some teacher's garage, and Linville came by, pulled my mother outside, and said, "The Country Gentlemen are looking for a drummer. Their drummer's gonna quit, and I think you should bring Kopana down." I wasn't really hip on it, because I couldn't drive yet. And at fifteen, man, you're not really up on hanging out with your mom anymore. You don't want your mom taking you to a gig, you know what I mean? It's just not cool.

So I didn't want to audition for the Country Gentlemen. For one, it was the whole "I don't want my mom dragging me off to the gigs! I want to drive myself!" Two, I didn't want to play country music. I had been playing honky-tonk stuff, lots of Waylon Jennings and Willie Nelson, with some Lynyrd Skynyrd southern rock, and lots of Eric Clapton's "Cocaine" kind of stuff thrown in, so I was getting my jollies at least somewhere among all that mess. But if you're going to play with the Country Gentlemen, it's straight-up traditional fall-over-in-your-beer, my-wife-left-me, my-dog-is-dead, she-took-my-truck, woe-is-me kind of country music.

But I went anyway. Linville said, "It's a professional gig—don't be stupid!" And I thought, "You've got to start somewhere." It's not like we're the cultural mecca out in West Liberty and you're suddenly going to be discovered playing in somebody's garage. You've got to do something to get out and go play and experience, you know? I'm into having experiences. So I went. It was interesting—and I hated every second of playing with those guys.

They were rude. I don't remember a single one of them smiling at me or even being nice to me. They were pissed off right from the beginning. Linville had brought them a girl. It was like, "What the hell were you thinking? We're called the Country Gentlemen!"

They all just looked at me and went, "Uh, yeah. You're pretty good for a girl. Sure do thank you for coming and playing, you did a real fine job," pat-pat on the back, and that was kind of it. And they sent Linville over, and Linville's story was that they liked me, they liked the way I played, everything was just fine, but they just couldn't have a woman in a band called the Country Gentlemen; it would have forced them to change the name. And they didn't want to change the name. But you know, all these guys in the Country Gentlemen, as I recall, were older, middle-aged guys, and probably some of them had grandkids as old as me.

Playing with the Country Gentlemen was the first instance that somebody had a problem with me being a girl who played drums. The first time somebody said that I couldn't do something because I was a girl. My parents never told me that. My family never told me that. The people at church never told me that. The people at the honky-tonk never told me that. My teachers never told me that! It didn't stop me. In fact, it's just one in a long line of big learning lessons. But it was the first time I had to deal with a negative reaction because of my gender.

Straight to Dorkland

ALI, VIDEO STORE CLERK, 31

When I was a kid, none of the guys on my school bus would let me join in their Dungeons and Dragons game. These games would happen at school during free time, and there was always one taking place on my bus route. The idea of getting to interact with monsters and casting spells seemed very cool, but the boys always had an excuse as to why I wasn't allowed to play—like, they were always in the middle of a campaign and couldn't add a new character in, or something had happened and they couldn't take on a new player. These boys were a tough group. One day Rob Humpsfeld was out sick, so they killed off his character. Rob came to school the next day, and the boys were like, "Rob, you're dead!"

So I didn't get invited to join a game, and I couldn't get my girl-friends to play the game or any other games with me. As much as I'd read the D&D book and had the figurines, you just can't play by yourself. I was really into board games or mind games. I had a smart group of friends, and none of us were into girly-girl stuff, but these girls still weren't into learning a bizarrely elaborate game like D&D.

Now, you have to flash forward a good twenty years to my the-ater group in Chicago, where there are a bunch of improvisers. The great thing about improvisers is they're all mostly geeks. You'll have a few frat boys, but mostly it's people who are very verbal, pretty smart, and very funny. So when this underground Dungeons and Dragons game started up at the theater, I ap-proached them very cautiously and quietly. They said that I seemed like the type of person who might be interested in the game, and I said, *Oh my God! Yeah!!!*" But there were too many people in line to join the game, so I got wait-listed.

When I was thirty years old, I finally got into the Dungeons and Dragons game. I play every Sunday and actually schedule my work hours around the game.

I picked a Welsh name for my game character because Tolkien based his Elves on the Welsh and also because even though I'm a "mutt," the biggest chunk of me is Welsh. So her name is Eirian, which means "silver." She's a fighter, because that's what the group needed—a fighter, pure muscle—so that was the condition of my getting in. It was weird at first, because I agreed to take a character who was very much against what my instincts were. But now I'm really glad I did. It's this whole new way of thinking. What my character wants to do is wade in with a sword, not talk, but just hack stuff to bits. That attitude is so different from the way I live the rest of my life that I love it! I spend so much time in life over little decisions, like, "Should I do this or that?" or "What are the ramifications?" or "How will this affect this relationship or social grouping?" I can't help thinking like that, so it's refreshing that there are three hours a week where my job is to wade in and tear stuff up! "Is it an Orc? [one of the humanoid monster villains in *The Lord of the Rings*] Yes. Kill it!" That's the extent of my logic.

Being this character makes me think about my body differently. A lot of the game is thinking about what your character *could* do in a situation. The more you play, the more skills you get; and the more likely you are to be able to do something, the harder you'll be able to punch. We were fighting some bad guys, bad snake-men, and one of them had cast a circle of darkness, a spell where suddenly you can't see anything. But one of my skills is blind-fighting, because I'm a warrior. I was on a wagon, and I was like, "Wait a minute! Can I jump off the wagon, tumble, and land in the light?" And the dungeon master thought about it and went, "Yeah, check your dexterity." Your dexterity score is how nimble you are, and then you roll a die, and if you get under that score, you get to do the thing you were trying to do. Higher dexterity gives you a better chance, but fate can always screw you up. When I'm this character, it occurs to me to try to "do" things. I don't normally think about my body in that way, but when I pretend to be this elf, I think, "Wait a minute! I have the physical skills to do that!" In real life I don't think to solve problems with my body. It makes me think about myself differently: Why don't I get into a yoga class or a martial arts class? It seems more plausible to me now. Punching and kicking can be cathartic and interesting!

Brute Love

ILENE, MEDICAL STUDENT, 26

I met hockey in sixth grade, when a *Highlights* magazine article awakened me to the exploits of the Edmonton Oilers. I remember the first broadcast I singled out to watch, remember being riveted by the players. I do not remember the first goal I saw, or the score of that first game. Just the uncommon grace of the sport.

From then on hockey was my dirty little secret. I would watch games late at night, making dives to the channel switcher whenever my grandparents entered the room, pretending to do my European history. What precisely embarrassed me, I do not know. Maybe it was the perceived misconceptions. Because even in my earliest stages of loving hockey, I realized the sport suffered from a public relations crisis. As a game that can border both on art and on organized crime, hockey's motto is still "Give blood, play hockey."

It's not as if I felt my friends or family would think my interest in the sport meant I'd become a thug overnight. I just had an irrational shame for watching. Hockey was for boys. No, hockey was for punks who couldn't think of anything more worthwhile to do with their time, kids like the guy next door who played street hockey in front of our house with ratty, matted old tennis balls and spat at cars when they honked for him to get out of their way. And even if hockey was for girls, I would've been the last girl it was for.

I grew up with a piano pedal to my foot and went to sleep reciting my multiplication tables. The very notion that sports could transcend life was not a philosophy my family would ever have recognized. Sports, for my parents, simply held no value. So I didn't have the guts to play sports. Instead, I watched.

In the beginning, I was a fan. Watching hockey was my chance to root for the good guys. The Oilers, of course, were the good guys. A year after I started watching hockey, the Edmonton Oilers captured their fourth Stanley Cup in five years. My heroes had won. I watched their victory in a darkened room with headphones so as not to wake my grandparents—the game had ended at midnight. I remember feeling that irrational sense of pride a fan feels at the success of their favored team—as if I had played some small role in their victory.

In the following years I found that I could only be a spectator for so long. Life gets in the way. My interest ebbed and waned, depending on my access to cable TV and online newspapers. By my freshman year in college, I had written hockey off in my mind as an adolescent phase. (What had I been thinking? Only a teen-ager could be so obsessed with a *game*.) So I barely blinked when one of my hallmates mentioned that our college had a women's ice hockey team that was inviting tryouts, even for inexperienced skaters. So in my junior year of college, having skated twice in my life, I decided that even after all these years, hockey still looked pretty fun. And it was.

I try and explain my love of hockey to those who love me: how I itch to put on a pair of skates, why I agonize over the ongoing exploits of the New York Rangers, why there are times when I'd rather watch a hockey game than go to a party, and why nothing would mean more to me than seeing my friends' and family's faces in the crowd as I skate my last game with my college's ice hockey club.

What none of them understand is how I am naked out on the ice. The game hides an unspeakable beauty. It's so hard to cap-ture in words the physical rush of adrenaline when you do a thing, *the* thing you love. The challenge and excitement of the game will never change for me. And it's this sameness that I find comforting, like the knowledge of an unconditional love.

First Field: From Wage Slave to Career Woman

CHAPTER 12

Barely Working

ELIZABETH, COMPUTER PROGRAMMER, 29

I was twenty-one, had just gotten back from living in England for a year, and had contracted mono. I lost all my energy so I couldn't really hold down a job. A friend of mine said she was taking a life drawing class and they needed models. This was at Southwest Missouri State University, where I was a student. She thought the job paid pretty well, and you basically just had to sit there. Since I was recovering from mono, I couldn't move anyway!

The first time I posed for the class, I wore this really great floor-length kimono. It was white cotton with big inky blue-black letters on it. So I came in wearing that, and I remember walking up to a chair at the front of the classroom, taking off my robe, and just sit-ting there. I knew some of the students, and I remember having to make myself sit still.

The class really liked how the robe looked, so my first pose was just sitting there with the robe half on and half off. I think I made something like eight dollars an hour. Minimum wage was under five dollars or something, so it was fantastic.

I modeled for a year, a year and a half. The first night was one of the easier nights, because after getting through the initial weirdness of people staring at my naked body, the truly hard part was holding a pose for a long period of time. That became hard on my body, hard on my back.

Also, as people got to know me, they got too familiar with me. One art professor would come up and just act like I was an object or something. I'd be completely naked in front of class, and he wouldn't touch me, but he would point to me and get his hands really close to my body, saying, "See how this shape looks. You should be shading it in this way."

A couple times things got uncomfortable. There was one person in the class who started laughing every time the instructor left. I remember he kept on laughing. I felt like I was in a very exposed position. I was curled up on the floor in almost a fetal position. And he kept on snickering, and I couldn't figure out why.

I felt really stupid doing the quick poses because you're just supposed to prance around. The first night I did that, it was awful. I mean, I would feel stupid enough doing that with clothes on! It's like playing freeze tag. I couldn't think of enough stuff to do. When I would pose still, I would redecorate my apartment. And I'd lose track of time, lose track of where I was redecorating.

The job got harder because I got to know the professors and some students. People would recognize me at the grocery store and wave. I thought, "I'm naked in everybody's living room."

That's when I had to stop. I think because I started becoming just the naked girl, and I didn't like that. I mean I *was* naked, but to the class, I was *just* the naked girl.

Paying Royalties
NANCY, AIR TRAFFIC CONTROLLER, 37

The day I turned sixteen, I marched into Burger King and filled out a job application. I was so thrilled to be working there. It must have been from watching the commercials. Everybody always looked like they were having such a good time.

On my first day of work, I made French fries. My uniform was a brown polyester dress, which was too short on me because I had such long legs, and a weird hat. It was a hideous outfit, but I didn't care. I was so happy, even if every night I went home smelling like grease. Working at Burger King was considered the coolest job you could get in high school. You were really popular because your friends came in and you could give them free food.

The employees got one free meal a day. Everyone had to make their own meal, so we all used to pile three or four patties on a bun, put lots of cheese and bacon on, maybe throw a chicken patty on top. It was great.

I bought jeans with my first paycheck. Whatever they were, they were the kind of jeans that had a lot of fancy stitching on the back pockets.

I worked at Burger King off and on for four years. After a while I started to get an attitude. The assistant manager didn't like me very much, probably because of this attitude. He was always trying to punish me by giving me really horrible tasks to do. The worst thing he did was when he gave me a razor blade and sent me outside to scrape the gum off the ground of the drive-through.

It was a really nice day, so I took off my stupid hat, and since I was wearing a tank top, I took off my top, and I rolled my brown pants up into shorts. So I was out there having a really good time, enjoying the day, scraping a little gum. The assistant manager noticed I was enjoying myself a little too much and sent me back inside to the deep fryer.

The scariest incident during my time there was when a busload of prisoners came by late at night. It was just me out in front, the assistant manager, and one kid in the back at the fryer. I was so scared, I'm sure the look on my face was one of pure fear. I didn't even want to turn my back to get their orders. The prisoners were perfectly nice, though. I'm sure they didn't care I was this sweet young girl in high school. They just wanted their hamburgers.

Quitting Time
NOELLE, GRADUATE STUDENT, 32

I have a history of not necessarily quitting but leaving jobs. My first time ever leaving a job happened the year I came back from France. I was twenty-two. I had used up all my money and loan potential in my year abroad. So I was working three jobs, and they were all crap jobs, but one of them was especially crappy. It was a telemarketing job. The worst thing about this one was they told you that it wasn't telemarketing. They told you that you were doing surveys to find out about school bonds and levies. The job was based in Missouri, but they were doing all these surveys for California. They told us that all we were doing was taking public opinion polls, that we were like a tiny little Gallup agency, and we were just taking polls, so we shouldn't feel bad about invading people's privacy, that we should think of ourselves as helping out with education in California.

Meanwhile we were going to be making minimum wage, and it was fine. But it wasn't fine, because as you read the surveys to people, you realized that what you were really doing was trying to generate quotes or statistics that would back a particular part of a campaign. So it was really telemarketing, and I felt that it was very unethical to call and say, "Do you think that building a school in an already crowded school district is a good idea?" Or "Do you think that XY school, which doesn't have a swimming pool, needs one?" And it was just a yes-or-no survey, so people couldn't voice any of their own comments; they just had to answer the questions. So basically, you got people on the phone and told them you were doing a public opinion survey, which was a big lie. Usually about halfway through the survey, they realized it was all a lie, and they started getting pissed off and tried to answer the questions in their own way, but there was no room for that at all. And of course we were monitored while we did this. They listened in on our conversations, so it had to be completely by the book. I'm not very good at by the book. I didn't realize that at the time, but I know that about myself now.

One time I got into trouble because I sort of let the interview turn into a conversation and said, "This is the way it has to be. I'm sorry, but if we can do this, that would be great." So I got pulled into the office, and the boss—they really thought they were going to be some kind of big-time agency—scolded me and threatened to fire me until I cried. In reality, they were just scraping by in hiring the amount of people they had, and they were trying to scare the shit out of us and make us feel grateful that we had a job at all so we would come back. Columbia, where I went to school, is a college town. There are lots of telemarketing places in Columbia. They come into town and take advantage of young, poor kids who don't know how they're going to survive, and that's what was happening to me.

After I got yelled at and made to cry, there was a part of me that felt like I had never been so humiliated in my life. I never had an experience where an employer told me off. I'd had a lot of bad jobs, but I usually did pretty well in them. After that a part of me realized that it wasn't my fault. Maybe I did something I wasn't supposed to do by not keeping exactly to the script, but the environment in this office was not good, and I had a feeling that it was unethical, but I was trying to convince myself otherwise.

I was working two other jobs, in a McDonald's and reading for a blind student on a tape, and I was a full-time student. So I was just exhausted all the time, stressed out all the time. One day I was driving to this telemarketing job—and this is truly reprehensible, but I'm not sorry. I just never made the turn. There was a place in the road where I was supposed to turn, and I just didn't and drove back home. And I thought, "What am I doing?" And my heart was pounding and my head was whirling. I didn't call, I didn't explain to them why, and I never went in again, and I never communicated with them again, though they called me several times, begging, pleading for me to come back. That's when I realized that my intuition had been right—that they were just trying to scare me. I behaved in a "terrible" way, and they were still *dying* to get me to come back. I never went in to pick up my last paycheck, I just didn't want any contact with them—and I desperately needed the money! I just let it go.

Jest for Fun
ANNIE, PSYCHOTHERAPIST, 67

I decided to be a clown, what, maybe four years ago? So I'm a come-lately clown. I've always loved humor, and when I speak on the subject of humor, one of the things I talk about is how we restrict ourselves to one little narrow definition of humor. So I'm always looking for new forms of humor. Well, I think clowning is a form of humor. And I decided that the best way to investigate that was to become a clown.

Her name is Cozy, and she has purple hair. She's a little bit ditzy, and she wears sort of a little coif hat. She wears pastel colors and is a very gentle clown. The clown is made up of what's inside of you, the parts inside of you that are most important. For me, it's gentleness, playfulness, and a little bit of ditziness—you know, just poking fun at self. I also sing a lot as a clown.

When you become a clown, you think like a clown. A couple of months ago I had become Cozy, and my partner Dale was taking pictures. I looked at him and said, "I think we need a picture of Cozy on the refrigerator." I climbed up to the top of the refrigerator." He took the picture of Cozy on the refrigerator, and of course we now have it hanging *on* our refrigerator!

I was clowning at the International Special Olympics in Raleigh, North Carolina, and so many parents would watch their little children walk right up to me, take a look, and kind of smile. The parents would say, "You know, she's always been afraid of clowns. I've never seen her like this!" Because the little children were comfortable, I felt about twelve feet tall!

Earning Your Stripes

SHIRLEY, RETIRED PRISON GUARD, 61

It was a rainy, cool spring day in March, and I had just turned eighteen years old. My dad, who drove a gravel truck, didn't haul on rainy days, and so on this particular day he drove me to school. Once he dropped me off, I hopped out of the car, ran into the school building, and immediately shot right back out through the side door.

I had a plan that day. I ran through the alley beside the Sweet Shoppe, down past Elam's Gas Company, and over the hill to the City Restaurant on Main Street. I saw the army recruiter's car parked right out in front of the restaurant.

I went inside and sat down on the stool beside the recruiter. I'm sure he could see the anxiety on my young, scared face. He asked me if I wanted to ask him something. I cleared my throat and said, "Yep. I want to go into the army." He asked my age and if I had my high school diploma. When I told him my age and that I had no diploma, he immediately told me to forget it.

After arguing with him a bit, I asked, "Ain't that your car parked out there on the street?"

"Yes," he said.

I said, "Whelp. I'll be in that car when you leave, even if I have to ride in the trunk."

My persistence paid off. The recruiter agreed to take me as far as Morehead (Kentucky) to take one test. He said if I passed it, he and I would come back to town and talk to my parents, get their signature on some papers, and then head to Ashland so I could take my GED test.

Let me point out that a young lady entering the military service in those early years, well, her reputation was pretty much tainted from the get-go. This was another struggle you had to overcome, if you so desired to hold your head high and let both males and females know just exactly who you were and what you would and would not tolerate.

I must say, I was scared and full of determination to reach this goal I had set for myself. I passed the test at Morehead, came home, got signatures, and went on to Ashland for three more days of testing. Before I knew it, I was sworn in and sitting on a train headed for Fort McClellan, Alabama.

Now I was alone and on my own—or so I thought. Boy, was I wrong. I was there by my own choice, but I sure wasn't on my own. I realized that every time Old Serg paced in front of us yelling at the top of her lungs, swinging her swagger stick and pounding it on the ground, telling us we were no good and we thought we were so smart but we didn't know nothing 'cause we had no mamas and she was our mama now and we would do exactly as Mama told us to do, whatever and whenever. Poor Old Serg. I swear she was so skinny, she looked like somebody's little humble granny. Why, give her a bottle of strawberry pop to drink, turn her sideways, and she'd look like a thermometer. She would never tell her age, but she had to have been at least sixty-five years old.

Basic training was six weeks of the most vigorous training I would ever have. We learned the basics of army life—like how to stand at attention, how to speak only when spoken to, how to dress, how to sit without getting wrinkles in our skirts and jackets, how to roll our clothes and place them in our footlockers, how to spit-shine our boots and dress shoes. We learned how to march, count cadence, and make our bunks so straight and tight that when the inspecting officer came by and dropped a quarter on the bed, that quarter bounced to the ceiling. And if it didn't? Your bed would be completely torn up and turned over by the officers, and you'd have to do it again until it was right.

We spent time in the classroom learning military history and military ways of life. We also spent time on the rifle range, learning to shoot, breaking down our weapons, cleaning them, and then putting them back together.

If only I had been given the chance, I feel that I could have made the army a career. But times were so different back then, and due to the fact that I was still under twenty-one, other people made my decisions for me. The army was going to send me to Europe, and boy if I didn't want to go, but my parents wanted me back home in Kentucky—where I've stayed ever since.

I had only two years of this wonderful career, and those two years have and will always remain in my memory. The pride I felt wearing my uniform is unexplainable. On the parade ground when we were marching, saluting "eyes right," as we passed the grandstand was just unbelievable. My heart was bursting with so much pride. There was a song that we would sing as we marched that went, "Duty is calling you and me. We have a date with destiny. Ready, the WACS are ready. Their pulse is steady, a world to set free. Service, we're in it heart and soul. Victory is our only goal. We love our country's honor and we'll defend it against any foe."

Singing that song, I felt that I was floating on cloud nine. I was the most important person on the face of this big, beautiful earth.

A Star Is Born
CATHY, CHARITY DIRECTOR, 44

I grew up on Long Island, always loving the movies. I remember seeing *Funny Girl* as a little kid and being totally transfixed. That movie changed my life. Between the performance and the story and the emotions—you name it, it hit every button for me. I was completely mesmerized.

I also always loved the theater. I remember my father taking me to see *Oliver*. He was a doctor, and one of his patients was part of the play's technical crew. After the show we got to go backstage to see the moving turnstiles and turntables on the stage. I was completely blown away. And there were all these little kids, my size and my age, who were the actors. So to say that the entertainment bug bit me at an early age is an understatement. But as a girl, I didn't know you could get a job in the entertainment business. On Long Island everyone was either in the wholesale garment business, or their fathers were doctors or lawyers—at least the people I knew.

I went off to Boston University and only lasted a year and a half there. I found going to BU was the same thing as going to summer camp or high school; all the kids were cut just like me. I really wanted to be in Manhattan, and after staging a protest and dropping out of school for six months, my parents finally consented to my going to New York University. I continued on my little path to study journalism, but at that point I got pretty serious about film. I started striking a very artsy pose and loving the downtown Village feeling.

When I graduated, I had to get a job, and the concept of moving to California to work in the movie business didn't seem like something I would do. People from New York don't tend to jump all over the country. New York's so great, why leave it? I really didn't have the burning desire to be a journalist, and if you don't have the burning desire to go into a field, then you're not going to succeed. One of my mother's friends had a daughter who worked for an ad agency that specialized in Broadway show advertising. The woman who ran the agency had an intern, a non-paid graduate student from Yale, working with her for six months. He got college credit, and basically he went everyplace she went. If she went to Joseph Papp's office, so did he. If she was in a recording studio, if she was in a meeting with a client, he was by her side. There was a lot of grunt work—he'd run out and get cigarettes or a bottle of wine—but that was a small price to pay for what he was exposed to.

I went into Manhattan to this agency, and I'm thinking, "I really don't want to be in advertising, but advertising is kind of like making thirty-second movies, so at least I can get exposure to that technique, and *it's Broadway*! We're not selling Twinkies or cars, we're selling theater, and I love theater." I walk in and interview with this woman Nancy, and she's absolutely wonderful and charming and smart and sassy and accessible. And of course she wants to hire me—I'm free labor. I'm totally presentable, I'm totally able-bodied and -minded, and I'm not going cost her a dime.

I call my father from the lobby of the building and say, "Dad, I was just offered a job." And he's ecstatic. And I say, "There's one catch: they're not going to pay me, I'm going be an intern." And he says, "But you finished school, what do you mean you're going to be an intern?" I make him a deal. "Why don't we look at it like this will be my graduate school? You paid for my undergraduate school, and this will be graduate school. If you cover my expenses, I'll live at home and commute into the city, plus I'll put a six-month cap on it. If they don't hire me, at least I'll have had practical experience in the work world, I can put it on my résumé, and I can get a job."

His sage advice is, "Just make sure they pay your commute ticket."

Dream Girls was one of the first accounts I worked on. Starting at seven at night, we'd go to a recording studio and cut music for the show's demo commercials. About an hour or so into the session, my boss would have a bottle of wine brought into the studio. She and the engineer would have a drink. I realized that we were not going anyplace for hours, and this was just part of the creative process. We'd finish at ten at night and go sit down at the Palm and eat steak and French fries. For me it was very, very glamorous—being in recording studios, cutting demos, going to restaurants late at night, then getting on the train and going back home.

I was loving every minute of this job, and I couldn't wait to get to work, and I was hating the fact that there were weekends. We were preparing for a big television commercial shoot for *Dream*

Girls. The musical hadn't opened yet, but it was going to be the undisputed hit of the season. We'd hired a very fancy-schmansy high-profile director to film the commercial for us and brought in all the other big, big hitters. The woman who was the agency producer left all the files containing the shoot's logistical breakdowns and budget work in a taxi.

And all I know is that I arrived at work in the morning all bright eyed and bushy tailed, ready for another exciting day, and my boss was fit to be tied. I don't remember if the producer was at the agency or at her apartment, but it was drama extraordinaire.

I was sent up to the producer's apartment to look for the files, and when I entered her apartment, her Abyssinian cat attacked me. The files weren't there, and nobody could find them anywhere.

This was the first real dramatic moment that I saw on the job. I'd been there a few weeks, totally thinking, "Everybody loves each other here! This is the best place in the world!" Now I was seeing the ugly reality of work: if you messed up, this was what happened.

That afternoon I'm called into my boss's office. I'm really nervous because it just hasn't been a good day at the ad agency. And she says, "Kid, I'd like to make you an offer. I'm going to give you a raise." I look at her and say, "But I don't get paid—how can you give me a raise?" And she says, "I'm going to give you four hundred dollars, and if you can do it, we want you to be our producer."

I'm feeling like the girl from *42nd Street*—"Kid, you're going out there a nobody and coming back a star." The windows of their office look out on Schubert Alley, and I'm looking at the sign for *A Chorus Line,* and I'm looking at the sign for *42nd Street,* and I'm hearing these words, and I'm like, "I'll do it!"

Before you could say, "Break a leg," I was producing TV commercials shown all over New York at the very young age of twenty-two. It was my first job, and it had so much energy and hokeyness and a tongue-in-cheek quirkiness that I fell in love from the minute I walked in the door.

A Brief Stint
JACKIE, PROJECT COORDINATOR, 39

My first job was at a photocopy store. This was during the prehistoric days before Kinko's and desktop publishing, so there was no do-it-yourself service. I was a sophomore in high school when my father informed me that he was no longer bankrolling my habit of Jordache jeans and cork wedges. I was hired at Quality Copies because I wasn't a pot-smoking eighteen-year-old boy—the store already had enough of those to spare.

I was put in the storeroom to open reams of paper and refill the copy machines. The two potheads, Bill and Ted, were glad to have someone to do their work. These two stringy-haired white guys fascinated me. As a young teen black girl, I studied them like an anthropologist studies a new civilization. Most days, while I worked, Bill and Ted debated who was the most bitching, Led Zeppelin or Pink Floyd. One afternoon they almost came to blows over the perceived gayness of David Lee Roth. I didn't know who or what they were talking about, and my opinion was never solicited.

Finally after weeks of working in the back with Bill and Ted (and getting a contact high from their clothes), I was brought up to the big leagues—the front counter to serve the copying needs of the public. It was actually a drag to spend hours copying customers' résumés, blueprints, and pages from textbooks, which was violating federal copyright laws. I was left alone one afternoon while my boss went on a break, and a guy in a wrinkled suit ran in needing a two-hundred-page legal brief copied in a hurry. He announced that he was an attorney, and I think he expected me to bow or genuflect, but I just grabbed his stack of papers and started the copy job. The copier machines we had were behemoths and very temperamental. I fed the first fifty pages of the legal paper into the copier with no problem. But as the copier got "hungrier," it started to eat the brief. I could swear the copier was making smacking noises. The lawyer started yelling at me and wanting to know what that noise was. I said, "Nothing," and started to remove the mangled original from the jaws of the machine. The lawyer saw what I was doing and jumped over the counter and grabbed the pages from my hand. Right then my boss came back—just in time to hear him call me an incompetent boob and ask me if I knew how long it took to type a two-hundred-page brief. Before I could say, "No, I don't, nor do I care," my boss took the pages and starting taping them back together. She calmed the now-apoplectic guy down and sent me to the storeroom to count inventory for the rest of my shift.

I knew this was going to be last thing I did at Quality Copies. When I returned to work the next day, I was told my services were no longer needed. I was relieved actually. I really wasn't cut out for the high-pressure world of photocopying.

First Family: Lessons Learned and Forgotten

CHAPTER 13

Baring Arms

GAIL, RADIO MARKETING DIRECTOR, 54

I was growing up in Memphis, Tennessee, my parents had just recently divorced, and my dad had custody of my older brother, who's five years older than me, my younger brother, who's thirteen years younger, and me.

One afternoon my dad and I were out putzing around, and we were driving back home. He was kind of hemming and hawing, like he wanted to tell me something. Finally he just said, "You know, we really need to have a conversation."

And I thought, "Oh God, I'm in trouble. What have I done now?" So I said, "Okay, what's going on?"

And he said, "What do you know about the birds and the bees?"

And I said, "Well, a little bit."

And at that point he pulled the car over and said, "Well, we need to talk about this, because you're getting to be a young woman now, and one of the things you shouldn't be doing at your age is wearing sleeveless blouses."

I had developed at an early age, with a pretty big-sized bust. His fear was that people could look down the side of my blouse and see my bra. That was the old southern thing that women covered themselves and you just didn't flaunt. But I thought he was crazy!

So I said, "What's the matter with wearing a sleeveless blouse?"

And he said, "This is part of our discussion. Do you know how men and women have babies?"

And I looked at him and said, "Oh yes, they screw!"

And he said, "Oh my God! Intercourse is the word! Intercourse! And when we get home, you're calling your aunt Sunny so she can tell you all about it."

Parental Consent

KATHRYN, PILOT, 28

A huge thing my mother did was to give me permission to enjoy sex. It was right about the time I started having my period, in the sixth grade. We were talking about how babies are made. We were in the car, and I'm like, "Mom, how long does it take for a baby to be made?" And she went, "Oh, I don't know, about five minutes."

The way she always handled things with me was to think about how she wanted to deal with a subject and then come back to it a little while later. So her punch line kind of ended the baby-making conversation, but about two or three hours later she thought about something she needed to say. "Kathryn, we need to talk about this," she said. "I just wanted to let you know that I want you to be responsible and be your own person, but as your mother, I also want you to know that I want you to enjoy sex." She was so worried because there are so many mothers out there who say, "Don't have sex because you'll get pregnant" or "It's a bad thing." But she said, "I just want to make sure that you know that I want you to enjoy sex, because it is a good and beautiful thing."

I was like, "Wait a minute! You can't come tell me that I can enjoy sex. You're my mother!" Then she told me that her mother told her the same thing!

Paging Dr. Killjoy
KRIS, ENVIRONMENTAL ENGINEER, 26

It's summer before senior year in high school, and I have just gotten up and am making my lunch to go to work. All of a sudden I get this horrible cramp in my side, like nothing I've ever had before. It hurts so bad, all I can do is sit on the floor. My mom is working at a doctor's office, so I call her. She hands off the phone to some nurses, so I can tell them what the pain is like. They all think it's appendicitis, so they tell my mom to pick me up and take me to a doctor.

We go to my regular family doctor, who asks some questions and does some kind of exam. He determines that I don't have appendicitis, but he's not quite sure what's going on. He asks me if I've recently been with a guy. I tell him yeah, and he's like, "I think it's probably an ovarian cyst, but I'm not positive. Since you have had sex, you should go to the gynecologist, and they'll check you out."

I tell him that I don't have a gynecologist because I've never been to one. And he says, "We need to tell your mom about this, so you're going to need to explain to her why you need to go to the gynecologist." And I go, "Oh man!" He's like, "Do you want me to tell her, or do you want to tell her?" I ask him to tell her that I have to go to the gynecologist and then have her come in to talk to me.

He goes out, and a few minutes later my mom comes walking in and she's like, "The doctor says you have to go to the gynecologist." And I'm like, "Yeah, Mom. Matt [who was my boyfriend at the time] and I have been having sex." She just sits there staring at me in frozen silence. She is in total disbelief. In a million years, I never would have imagined that this was the way my mother would find out about my sex life.

So we go off to the gynecologist, and he figures out that I have an ovarian cyst and that it is turning and that's why I'm in so much pain. He tells me, "This is not something that you can get from having sex." At that point I'm like, "Oh my God! You mean I didn't have to tell my mother?!"

The doctor puts me in the hospital for the night because I've gotten really dehydrated. While my mom and I are sitting in the waiting room, she decides to call my dad to tell him what's wrong with me. There's a phone on the table next to us, so she calls my dad, and he answers the phone and she just bursts out, *"Our daughter is having sex!"* There are about thirty people in the waiting room who hear this, and everyone just looks over at my mother and me. I'm sitting there, turning bright red, and wishing I were dead.

Motherf*&ker
KATHY, CABLE TV HOST, 45

I'm twenty-nine years old, and I've just purchased my dream car from years, years, and years back. It's a 300ZX. Black with a t-top, the whole nine yards. Nissan. Real sporty two-door-type car. My mom and dad are down to help me with my upcoming wedding in south Florida. My mother and I must have been running errands. So we're scooting around in this hot little car, and we're at a traffic light, and the next thing I know someone rear-ends me. The first word out of my mouth is *"Fuck!"* And rather than worry about my brand-new car or the excruciating pain in my neck, I look at my mother, and I go, "Oh Mom, I'm so sorry. I used the f-word!" Those are the first words out of my mouth. I'm like, "My God, what have I said to my mother!" And she's grabbing her neck going, "Oh, my neck!" So I guess she never even heard it, but here I am apologizing in the middle of the car wreck for saying a naughty word.

After the hit we get out of the car and investigate the accident, get all the preliminaries and the police reports—the whole nine yards. At the time I'm also smoking cigarettes—I haven't smoked since 1990—but I say, "Mom, I'm twenty-nine years old, I'm getting married in a couple of days, I've got to light this cigarette up." She knows I smoke, but I never smoke in front of her, so it's never talked about. And she says, "You just go right ahead!"

It might not seem like an important story, but you have to understand that in my family there wasn't drinking, there wasn't cussing, there wasn't yelling and screaming. We were kind of like the Tennessee version of an *Ozzie and Harriet* or *Leave It to Beaver* type family. Nothing wrong with that, but we respected our parents and we didn't say cuss words. And we definitely didn't smoke in front of our parents.

So saying the f-word was a real passage for me. It was a hump, another level of relationship with my mother. All of sudden I wasn't her little girl anymore.

Role Reversal

ANDREA, ALUMNI DEVELOPMENT OFFICER, 30

I was attending the University of Richmond and decided that I would go to France to study abroad for a semester. Southern

France is much more laid back and not as uptight as northern France, so I thought Avignon would be a fun place to be. In just two months I was living in an apartment by myself, knew the parish priest, and knew where to get my favorite American delicacies in the grocery store, and I felt like I had definitely come into my own.

While I was there, my parents came to visit; my father had a business trip to Florence, and they came over on a train. My older sister had just announced that she was pregnant, so my mother and I decided to go shopping for baby clothes. We didn't know if it was a boy or a girl, so we were kind of shopping for both. As we walked around the village, we found this adorable, stereotypically French children's clothing store, and we walked in. My mother started perusing on one side of the store, and I was on the other side. After a while my mother had found two pairs of baby booties that she wanted to buy. One pair was pink, one blue.

She went up to the counter. Now, my mother is a very, very strong woman. She is extremely self-confident, and we always say that we turned out to be the adults we are because of her. She was very much the disciplinarian. We always followed her lead. She was somewhat controlling but in a good way, she pushed us, and we always looked to her for guidance. So that's a side note to this epiphany I had. My mother approached the counter, very confidently. My parents were the stereotypical American tourists and often were like bulls in a china shop. They just went in and did whatever they felt comfortable doing, which often gave me some agita. But it was fine; I let her do her thing. And so she went up to the counter, and as she was buying the booties, the woman said to her, *"Deux pacquets?"* which means, "Two packages?" And my mother didn't understand what the woman was saying. I heard it going on, and I didn't even turn around, because to me, my mother knew everything. It didn't even occur to me that she might not understand what this woman was saying, didn't even occur to me that she didn't understand French, because in my mind, I really felt like there wasn't anything she didn't know.

And so from across the store my mother turned to me. I wouldn't say she was panicked, but she did look concerned. I looked back at my mother and said, "What is it?" And she said, "What did that woman just say?" And I said, "You didn't understand that?" And she said, "No!" Then it clicked in my head: obviously she didn't understand—she didn't speak French!

I walked over to the counter and said to the woman, *"Oui, deux pacquets,"* which means, "Yes, two packages." My mother said, "Oh! That's what she meant."

At that moment I had an experience where I thought, "Oh. My. God! For the first time, not only am I in a place that is so much more my own place than my parents', but my mother actually is looking to me for guidance."

Honestly, I had never thought in a million years that I'd ever have that moment. It showed me that I was in a place in my life where, yes I had left my family geographically and gone and developed a relationship with another culture, another place. But as soon as I was back in my parents' presence, I still felt that they were my guides, my anchor. That moment in the shop really made me realize that not only had I matured and had the ability to give my parents guidance, but also for the first time, my mother had felt comfortable looking to me for guidance.

From that moment forward, our relationship did change. Since then I've had the confidence to second-guess her, or to engage her in conversations about things she might not be so sure about. I've also felt like I could do more than that. We've had a couple instances where my mother was very ill and I ended up being her caretaker, watching her, making sure that she took her medicine, and learning not to push too hard. I think that if I hadn't had that experience in France, I wouldn't have felt as comfortable taking control of the situation. So that's kind of how I evolved.

First Farewell: Leaving Home, Breaking up, Saying Good-bye, and Moving On

CHAPTER 14

On a Roll

SHERRI, ACTRESS/MODEL, 28

My mom saved all of the voice mails that I left her when I started looking for my own house. She has every message from "Mom, you need to pray for me" all the way through to "I'm a home-owner!" It was really dramatic.

Long story short, I started looking for a place to live. I'd find a place that was a reasonable price but the size of a pea. As an actor and a model, there are weeks when I make decent money, and then there'll be weeks when I don't make squat. I have an awful lot of savings, because I'm real scared if anything like September 11 ever happens again, I need to be buffered. So I had a

friend look at my money and she said, "I think you can do this."
I got a loan and started looking. I looked all over Virginia, since I
grew up in Virginia, thinking I wanted to live there. I looked at ten
places with bums on the corner, broken glass in the parking lot.
And I thought, "This is not living." I didn't know what to do. So I
started praying about it.

I found a place online that I thought was cute, so I met the real
estate agent the next morning and had a look at the place. I kept
driving through the neighborhood going, "I can't afford this! I
can't afford this!"

There were these beautiful trees everywhere, a huge ballpark
and soccer field, and a cute, tiny neighborhood shopping area
with a little restaurant and a place to do your hair.

I had a bunch of rules. I had to have a place where I could have
a garden. I had to have two bedrooms because I have an office
and I'm sick of having my office and my bedroom in the same
room; that's ridiculous. The layout had to feel really good. It had
to feel safe.

I walked in and went, "Lord, this is where I'm supposed to live,
isn't it?" And I breathed a heavy sigh, because the doors were
really old on the closets, and the trim was going to have to be replaced all around the floor, and the bathroom was *ugly*, and the
kitchen was *horrible*, but the spacing was really great, and it was
nestled in the corner on the basement level of the townhouse—
I'd lived in basements for so long. I'd have my backyard with my
flowers and my little tree out there. I'd have my safe little corner,
with neighbors above me, beside me, both ways, so if I ever
needed help or the bogeyman ever came, I could knock on the
door and someone would be there. I liked that idea.

So I bought the place. I couldn't believe I did it, because I'm
really terrible about turning in applications and crap like that, but
I got the place, moved in, and I guess a few weeks after I moved

in I was at my gym, working out, late one night, and I went to the grocery store at midnight, which is typical for me because it's the only time I have off and the only time there aren't a lot of other people at the store.

I needed toilet paper, and I got the biggest daggone toilet paper collection I could get: a twelve-pack of Angel Soft. The biggest one they make, with like three across, and then four up. I even told the front counter woman, "This is toilet paper for my new house!"

I marched out of the store with the toilet paper tucked up under my chin and began skipping to my car like a twelve-year-old. It was the best feeling because I knew that this was toilet paper that I was buying for *my* house. I was so excited!

As much as owning a house makes me feel grown up, I play in it all the time. I turn on the radio and dance. My mom calls it "jukin'." I've allowed myself to be more myself in this place. I come in every day, and I say, "Hi, little world!"

Sticks and Stones
IRENE, HOMEMAKER, 72

I was born in Iwjer, Poland. In 1939 the Russians came to us and they put us in a ghetto. The ghetto was all around, surrounded with the iron. And every morning—I was not old, not young, I was already twelve years old—I used to go to work. I would go to the gate, and they used to say, "Who's here?" And they used to send us to work. They sent us on the street to sweep. One time they sent us far away from the house to a big building that was full of potatoes. We had to peel the potatoes. And we didn't resist because we had to do it, we had no choice.

This was how it was until 1941, in January. Then we ran away to live in the woods. Me, my father, my mother, my brother, and my sister. We lived all over, for three years, until we joined this other group in the woods. It was like a camp, where all the young people had rifles. There were about twelve hundred people. Not all young ones. Young ones, children, men, women, all kinds of people. This was in the woods, in Belarus.

In our camp all the mature men used to go to the small towns and steal food to bring back to the families who were hiding. My mother used to cook for a lot of people in the same bunker where we were sitting.

When the Russians sent the Germans away from Russia, these Germans were running through our woods. We caught three Germans, and they said, in German, "So many Jewish people still living?!"

We were all angry. We were very angry. Because they said, "So many Jewish people still alive?!" It was practically like these men, they spit on our faces. So everybody started to kick them and beat them and beat them.

We were standing in a circle, and everybody, they did what they wanted to do. Not everybody was there, because a lot of the people were out getting food. I'd say at least a couple of hundred people were in the circle. We beat all three of them and then we left them there.

Of course, I helped. For me, it was not very pleasant, but they killed us, why should we leave and not kill them? Listen, in such a time, you don't think too much. You act more than you think.

Listen, to tell you the truth, I couldn't imagine anything like this could ever happen. This is unbelievable to tell and to hear myself say it.

Everybody has a story.

Foreign Exchange
NELL, TEACHER, 33

When I was twenty, I spent my junior year abroad in France. Before I left, my mom, who had raised me in a very devout Catholic home, wanted me to promise her that I would go to church and get situated with a church right away. It was a very big deal for her—she didn't want me to go atheist in a very secular country. So the first thing I did when I went over was to go to mass, immediately. There was a church right near my dorm, and I talked to the priest and introduced myself, just like I would have done in an American Catholic church. And the priest was completely uninterested and very cold. He just didn't seem like he cared, and I wasn't prepared for that. I felt really disenchanted, and I tried going back a few times, but eventually I met a woman who invited me to go to her church, which turned out to be an Evangelical Protestant church—fundamentalist, I would say.

Not a lot of people in Nancy (the town where I was living) spoke English, and I didn't speak any French when I first got there. So meeting someone else who spoke English was really great! At first the friendship felt really homey and endearing because she had this fabulous French apartment in an old part of town, and I would take the bus and go down there and eat dinner with her, and we would talk about the Bible, and I felt that it was really special.

We were both in the same program, taking French as a foreign language, but I was at the very beginning level and she was a couple of levels ahead. She had majored in German, had gone to this great school, already knew one language, was twenty-two, and had already graduated from college. She was just hanging out in France, and I thought all of that was just so cool. Very gradually, she just sort of invited me into her life, and I felt very flattered and honored.

I started going to church with her. I was already very receptive to the idea of going to church, because of my upbringing. With her, I just kept getting more and more involved in the church. But there was this bone of contention between us—because, in a sense, she forced me to attend church with her. And I will say forced, because even at the time this happened, I felt sort of forced into talking about when I was saved, just to prove to her that I really was saved, that I really accepted Jesus Christ as my personal savior. And there was all this language that I didn't really understand. But I was kind of willing to go through with it because I thought, "This is what it takes to be her friend, and this is what it takes to have an active faith-life in this country, so I'm going to do it."

Eventually, I told her that I was never going to leave the Catholic Church, and as soon as I got back to America, I was probably going to go back to mass. But for now I would stay in her church. She put a lot of pressure on me in various ways to renounce the Catholic Church and to come into her fold. She had her own Bible study group in her home, and she organized her own activities for people she thought needed additional guidance; they went on skiing trips and retreats and all kinds of stuff. I realized eventually that she was like a one-woman ministry.

About halfway through the school year, the invitations started to taper off. I realized that she had decided that I wasn't going to be saved, or if I was, it wasn't going to be through her. Even though she claimed that we were still friends, I wasn't seeing her anymore. It hurt my feelings so much. I realized that I was just a guinea pig or a salvation tool. I realized that things were deteriorating between us. The last final hurtful thing for me was that she organized a big ski trip over the Easter holidays, which are two weeks long in France, and she didn't invite me because I wasn't French, I wasn't one of the missionary leaders, and I was Catholic.

I was a bad influence at every level. And I wasn't really a person to her.

When I went back home in July, she moved from France and was doing missionary work in a Spanish-speaking country. It was very clear to me that what she was interested in was being a missionary, and that people were not people to her. They were just souls—whatever she thought a soul was.

I handled it really badly. I should have written her a letter and said, "I'm sorry, but our belief systems don't coincide and I can't continue this friendship." But instead I just never returned any of her letters, and eventually she gave up and I was glad. But I always had a little regret about the way I handled the situation. As I prepare to get married, simultaneously cleaning my house and cleaning out my life, I've been looking up old friends on the Internet. I looked her up and found, in a very conservative Christian discussion group, one of her posts. She was lecturing someone—using the Bible as her authority—about how in vitro fertilization was against the laws of God. And someone else had written in and said, "I've had that done, and I think it's a blessing." All these conservative Christians trying to decide whether you should force the reproduction issue or not, and she, more than anyone else, was just completely sure she was right, saying, "This is what I've read, I know the Bible better than anyone else, this is how it is."

In other words, I felt like she hadn't changed at all. And I thought, "I'm so glad I let her out of my life—or forced her out of my life." Because she never did anything really but make me feel bad about myself. I've done it since then, and I think I've done it better, but that was the first time that I realized someone wasn't good for me, and I made a unilateral decision to end the friendship. And I'm not sorry at all, even though I did have some guilt, but now that's all gone. She's just the same self-important, proselytizing, pompous ass she always was.

My Way or the Thighway

DEE, ROMANCE WRITER, 40

Tom and I had gone to high school together and were boyfriend and girlfriend off and on through high school, but not college. We went to different colleges, and he would occasionally send a letter, wanting to get in touch—How are you? How are things going? Also, his best friend was a very good friend of mine. So all through college I would occasionally hear from his best friend that Tom was asking about me.

After college Tom called me. We were both back on Long Island, and he heard through mutual friends that I was back home, too. We started seeing each other. Less than six months later we were engaged. He proposed in a restaurant at dessert. I remember people applauding, but I also remember going back to my parents' house and my father looking absolutely stricken by the news—I had caught a look that I was not supposed to see. My parents always felt that Tom was a nice person, but my mother always said he was not a smart person. My father thought we didn't have enough in common to keep a relationship going. Here's an example: I love to go to movies and to the theater, and I love books. Tom was very threatened by anything cultural. One evening he wanted to go see *The Three Amigos* and I wanted to see *Blue Velvet*. We went to see *Blue Velvet*, and he sat through the whole thing going, "This is sick! This is really sick!" And then we went to *The Three Amigos*, and I got up after forty minutes and said, "I'll meet you at the bookstore afterward." I couldn't endure that movie.

As disappointed as my father was in Tom, Tom's mother was just as disappointed in me. I was not thin, and I did not wear makeup and big gaudy gold jewelry like she did. So she had a hard time relating to me. I remember being simultaneously intimidated by her, her dedication to her body, and how great she looked, and hating her for it at the same time. When she suggested Jazzercise to me, I thought, "This sounds like fun, I'll go." She picked me up in her Chrysler LeBaron, and I'm wearing sweats and a big T-shirt because I'm feeling like shit about myself, and she's in this perky little leotard. I go into Jazzercise, and I was younger than everyone by twenty years, so it's lots of ladies with long nails and big hair, in the Long Island VFW hall doing dance steps to Michael Jackson's "Wanna Be Startin' Somethin'?" I'm in a surreal hell. But I kept doing it because she was so happy that I was there with her, she was bringing me around, "I want you to meet my daughter-in-law." So I was willing to squelch my horror for acceptance. That was a big part of my relationship, squelching myself because I was so afraid of being alone.

I think I subconsciously sought out someone who would confirm how shitty I felt about myself. Tom—even his mother—definitely reflected back to me all the hatred I had for myself. So when Tom and I moved in together, we almost immediately began fighting because he wanted to watch *The Flintstones,* or we were eating dinner and he didn't want me to eat the rolls.

Things sort of came to a head on Valentine's Day. Tom had sent me flowers at work, and I got home and I was all excited because I was thinking we had made plans to go out to dinner—I wasn't going to have to cook. Tom was already home and had a big box of chocolates waiting for me. So I was thrilled, thinking that I must look fine if he's giving me these fattening things. Then he handed me the next gift. I opened it and saw a video called *Thinner Thighs in 30 Days.* I was stupefied. I didn't say anything. He looked at me and said, "Whaaaat?" I said, "I can't believe you did this." And he was like, "What? What? You're in Jazzercise now. You're always talking about losing weight." I said, "How can I lose weight if you give me a two-pound box of chocolates?"

I started to cry, and he did not understand at all. I remember thinking, "This person who says he loves me is sending me mixed messages. This person who is supposed to love me unconditionally clearly loves me conditionally." I think something clicked in my head at that point.

Up until then I had been making excuses. I had been making excuses the entire relationship. I think very often people know when things aren't right, but they're afraid. What will people think? "Oh my God, we've already lined up the caterers, I bought my dress." Or "I'll hurt him so badly that people will think I'm awful." Or "What if this is really the one, and I'm just having pre-marital jitters and I let it go and I never find anyone else?" For women in our culture, there's so much emphasis on being part of a pair that I think there is a terror in being alone.

I went into therapy before I called off the wedding. I can remember the therapist saying, "You have a choice: you can make him happy, or you can make yourself happy. And hurting him is unavoidable." I was terrified that everyone would hate me for calling things off just one month before the wedding. But I tried to imagine growing old with him, and I couldn't. I remember breaking up with him and saying, "We both have a right to be as happy as we possibly can be, and I don't think that that's going to happen together." Tom went totally ballistic. He was like, "How can you do this to me?!" He discouraged me from going into therapy, because I think he could see the writing on the wall. I think he had a strong sense that underneath it all I was unhappy.

When I broke up with Tom, my mother said, "I was going to give it one more month, and then I was going to ask you to post-pone the wedding—because you're not happy, and I can see that."

Tom's already on his second marriage. He's on Long Island, teaching. He had a son with his first wife, and they got divorced.

Now he's married to someone else he went to high school with. I'm sure he's still watching *The Flintstones*.

Homing Instinct
THIDA, ADMINISTRATIVE ASSISTANT, 40

I came to America from Thailand when I was twenty-eight. At the time I wanted to see something different. My older sister was living in Maryland, and she told me it was going to be very tough for me to move here. She said, "Some people make it, some do not."

The company I had worked for in Thailand helped buy my ticket, and so on June 1, 1992, I stepped onto American land in the Los Angeles airport. I stayed with my aunt for a week, and then I came to Maryland to be with my sister. I stayed in the house for a whole month, watching television and learning how to speak English better.

My first year was a tough time for me. One incident that I'll never forget happened in a store. I was having trouble figuring out the cash in order to pay for something, and I was struggling at the register, trying to figure things out. This lady standing behind me in line said, "Why don't you go back to your own country?" I was so stunned, I couldn't say anything. After I left the store, I kept crying and crying.

When I learned more about American life, I realized I had to stand up for myself in order to be accepted. If I let someone else step on me, they would step on me all the time.

It took me three years to get the courage to speak up. It happened when I was in a department store. Some lady told me to go back to my own country, and I just couldn't keep quiet anymore. I said, "I came here because the U.S. government allowed me to come here. I'm here legally, and you have no right to tell me to go home."

In that moment, I could see it in her eyes: I'm proud. I'm here.

Finishing School
RAE, CHILDREN'S BOOK PUBLICIST, 27

The August before sixth grade was kind of golden. I was a tomboy, and I mainly hung out with my best friend (another tomboy) and the boy next door. We did kid stuff, went swimming, played make-believe, toilet-papered other kids' houses, and were very serious about weird things like crushes, secret pacts, and who could run fastest. We also were a bit aware that things were going to change. We shaved our legs (not because we really needed to), talked about boys, wondered what having pubic hair would be like, and talked about how to be more feminine and popular. I think we actually made a secret pact to act more girly and be more popular.

Then school started, and we were suddenly in junior high, and she became more girly and popular, and I was the dissed outcast. In fact, it worked out that she dumped me and rallied the entire grade of eighty-some eleven- and twelve-year olds against me. It was hard enough not having a best friend anymore, but even worse having people actively pick on you all the time for no reason. And no matter how much I knew that they all sucked, and I really was cool, and was doing cool things and dressing and thinking in ways I liked, it still sucked to get up every day knowing they would make fun of me nonstop all day, from the bus stop to the crank calls at night. And it still hurt.

Basically, I felt like I was in a fog, banging my head against a wall, and trying to deny that I was upset and hurting all the time. I slept a lot, a lot, a lot. I was wondering when things started being like this, and if I would be this unhappy all of my life, or at least for all of junior high. My parents knew something was up, but I was way too embarrassed to tell them about it. My older sister knew something was up, and I started hanging out with her instead of the kids my own age.

I don't really remember too many specifics about that year. I switched to a private all-girls school for seventh grade, along with my former best friend, who was really getting disgusted at how mean she was being and how different she was acting than she wanted to act. Things got better.

But if I ever run into people I knew from that time, especially the girls, I don't play the happy-to-see-you game. Even if they're nice people now doing interesting things, I somehow cannot forgive them for being as mean and stupid and hurtful as they were fifteen years ago. They made me into a different person.

Brush With Death

LAURA, SOFTWARE DEVELOPER, 39

I saw my first dead body when I was fourteen. It was January 1978. Two years before, I had moved from a D.C. suburb to a small town in the mountains of southwestern Virginia. We lived in an old farmhouse on a dirt road, and our closest neighbor was about half a mile away; the town of a thousand residents where I went to school was ten miles away. I was in the middle of nowhere, with one traffic light in town and three television channels. There was absolutely nothing to do.

The transition from suburban to rural life was difficult, and I was miserable living there until a girl my age moved in with her grandmother, who was one of our closest neighbors. She'd grown up in Houston and San Antonio, so like me, she felt like a fish out of water in rural Virginia. Unlike me, she'd had (or at least claimed to have had) a fairly wild life, including experimenting with alcohol, drugs, and sex. Kathy became quite the influence on me. I actually experienced many of my firsts with her—getting drunk, smoking cigarettes and pot, and making out with a guy.

School was closed most of that January because it snowed almost incessantly. We soon tired of sledding, watching the limited offerings on TV, and smoking the cigarettes we stole from my stepfather. One day we bummed a ride into town with my parents on their way to work. After a few hours of wandering around town and hanging out at the local fast-food restaurant, we got bored. We had already visited the few shops in town, and about the only place left to visit was the funeral home.

It was actually Kathy's idea, but of course, every idea she came up with I eagerly went along with because I was so eager to shed my goody-goody image. We walked right into the place, and Kathy said to the funeral director, "We'd like to see a dead body."

The funeral director didn't know what to make of us. He paused and just stared at us, then asked if there was someone in particular we wanted to see. When we told him no, he looked completely flabbergasted, but he led us into a dimly lit viewing room and then left us alone.

It was like we were drawn to this body. We walked up to the open casket, where a waxen-looking man lay. He was maybe in his fifties, with steel-gray hair and sunken cheeks. I remember thinking that his skin wasn't too wrinkly. He was wearing a dark gray suit.

We were so revved up on adrenaline, like we knew we were doing something kind of bad. We stood looking at the body for a few minutes, giggling nervously, waiting for the body to jump out at us, but of course, the body didn't move. Finally, Kathy said, "Should we touch it?" We each brushed his cheek for like a split second and then hightailed it out of there.

I knew it was a weird thing to do, that it was nothing to brag to my friends about. I never told anyone about it, not even my brother. I think this is the first time I have even thought about it since I was fourteen. It's not like the experience traumatized me or gave me nightmares. It wasn't like I knew the man, so it didn't feel as real. I think it was less about seeing death than my feeling more alive by the experience. In some strange way this guy was dead, and I was standing there, heart beating wildly, synapses firing, giggling like an idiot. Man, I was alive.

Among the Living

KERSTIN, MASSAGE THERAPIST, 28

When I was in the sixth or seventh grade, I really hated my parents, but I mostly hated my dad, because he was the mortician. I hated him for having this profession; I thought that I was cursed in some way. I wasn't able to be a kid when I was a kid. There were families coming in to look at their departed, or there were funerals going on downstairs, or Dad was on the phone and it was "the call." When you're a kid, you want to run around and scream and yell and get into things. But at our house it was always, "Shhh! There's a family downstairs!"

As I got a little older, I decided, fine, since my friends were always asking me, "Have you seen this or seen that?" I decided I was going to take a look at every gross thing that came through our door. I had seen dead people but nothing horrible. Dad would keep me out of the morgue if there was someone who'd lost their head in an accident or had shot himself in the face. But if they were just pretty regular deaths, he'd be like, "Come on in!"

My dad never wanted to make looking at death a weird thing. He had a philosophy. I completely agree with it now, but at the time I thought it was pretty strange. His philosophy was: you're only afraid of death because you're taught to be afraid of it. He thought it was crap that people were constantly coming in to the funeral home and getting freaked out, and he enjoyed messing with them. He didn't understand why people would get so freaked out by things that weren't going to harm them in any way, shape, or form. It's not like dead people can jump up and get you.

I remember one time the town coroner had come to our house and told my mom that there was a case involving a gentleman who had started stabbing his wife with a tire iron. He'd come home to tell his wife that he didn't want a divorce and started beating her with the tire iron and then eventually started stabbing her with it. He chased her over to the neighbor's front porch, where he continued stabbing her. He had to stop only because the tire iron had gotten lodged in her heart and her bones were so shattered. She was left to die on the porch. The couple had an eighteen-month-old who was asleep in their home. So he went back home. The neighbor eventually found the wife on his porch and called the police. There was a SWAT team surrounding the house, and they were talking to the husband on the phone when they heard a giant explosion. The police didn't know if he had hurt the baby or if he was sending off a warning shot. They stormed the house and found out that the guy had put a rifle in his mouth and pulled the trigger. My dad said when he got to the scene, he noticed, about fifteen feet away from the body, on the opposite wall, this plaque with the wedding vows on it. Dripping down from it was blood and brain matter and fragments of skull.

That image just struck my attention, and I decided that I was going to take a look at this guy and see what he looked like. The idea of there being life in a body in one second and then no life in a body like ten seconds later just seemed so incredible to me.

I had always heard my dad talk about people shooting themselves in the head and how it took certain guns to do the job. I thought that if you shot yourself with a gun, your head would come off anyway. But Dad explained there are certain types of guns, and some people have an entrance and an exit wound and some people don't have a head at all. It always shocked me, and I was so intrigued by the idea, I had to see it.

When the coroner opened the body bag, I was right at the door of the morgue, which was where the head of the table was situated. He opened the body bag from the head down. He had said that there was absolutely nothing left of his face, but the investigators had picked up all the little skull fragments and all the teeth and stuff that they'd found in the room and piled it on top of his chest. So when he opened the bag, there was this—I don't want to use the word *gooey*—but this red, kind of wet mass, I suppose. And it was so weird to see, you know, a fully dressed body, with what I think was part of his bottom jaw and his ear on one side, and then the other ear sort of dangling. His shoulders were soaked in blood. I stood there trying to figure out where his head and face would have been. The coroner was pointing out where the one ear was, and he showed me where a little piece of the chin was. It was just a piece of the chin, and some molars. The rest of the teeth were piled up on the chest.

I couldn't wait for his body to be out of my house. The family wound up cremating him, but he had to be at our house a day or two because the investigation wasn't over and his mother was trying to decide what to do with his body. So just the thought of him being in my house . . . I guess there is a whole psychological thing to it. The more I hear stories about people who have died, the more intrigued I am about seeing them when they're dead. I think it's the method-actor thing, where I look at their face and try to figure out what kind of life they led. I think about whether they have family, who's going to miss them, what kind of devastating loss it was for somebody—or for nobody even. When I know more about how they died, I want to know them even more. There's an irony: you want to know them more, but you can't. It's almost romantic. I may be inventing a better life for that person.

I think I kept looking at dead people because there is a piece of me trying to get away from feeling afraid of death. I am deathly afraid of death. And no matter how many bodies I saw, the looking still didn't make me any less afraid. I just wanted the hell away from death, I wanted to stop talking about it, to stop looking at pictures of caskets. I wanted none of it. I wanted to live! I wanted to stop thinking about something that was hopefully very far away for me.

My father retired two years ago, so I don't see dead people anymore. But working at a newspaper in the classifieds section, I'm continually taking death notices, and that depresses the shit out of me. I'll start thinking, "Who was this person? What was their life like?"

I don't go to a lot of funerals—I'm not that morbid! The most recent one I went to was a friend of mine who was killed in a car accident. His name was Justin. That was the first time I realized what my dad's job meant to other people and that allowed me to come to peace with him.

My friend and his family were coming back from vacation, and he and a few of his friends were in a car about fifteen minutes ahead of his brother and his parents' car. His car had gotten into an accident, and he was the only who was even remotely injured, and he died. His family drove up onto the scene a few minutes later.

It was absolutely unbelievable because this kid had so much life. (You always say that about people; when people die—you only point out the good things about them. But why can't you do that when they're alive?) Before his body was sent to our funeral home, the home that first took care of the body didn't do a very good job, according to my dad. There was a lot of swelling in his face and it didn't look like him, so my father tried to talk the parents out of seeing their son, but he understood their need to see him. A more tragic part of the grief process is not being able to see the body and say good-bye. So my father did his best and his parents saw him, but no one else did. The funeral was closed casket.

I remember watching that casket and thinking my friend was going to come walking in and it was going to be a big joke. It was ridiculous to me and I was sobbing and sobbing and I was more upset than I could have imagined. I turned around and saw my dad in the back of the room and thought, "I am so glad that my dad is the one who is comforting this family. He is the one who is giving them the answers about how long he suffered before he died. He is the one who made it okay for them to be able to see their son, and he is the one who will be there for them whenever they need him to answer questions and make decisions when making decisions is the last thing they want to be doing."

So I finally made peace with my father and his job. It wasn't about touching dead people or dressing them or making them look peaceful. It was about dealing with the people who are left behind. He knew how to do the stuff that people normally consider disgusting—that was just part of the job. Whenever I asked him why he became a mortician, his answer was always, "Because I wanted to help people." And that didn't make sense to me until Justin's funeral. I'm very proud of my father now, of how I grew up. I hold it like a medal.

Death with Father

HOLLY, EDITOR, 29

I remember the first time I saw my dad in his open casket. He looked handsome, like Ned Beatty. I was standing with my older sister Rachael, who looked in and said, "If he hadn't given me this sick sense of humor, I'm not sure I could handle this." I was twenty-two and already the mother of a toddler.

Rachael and I stood there for a while, trying to come up with something appropriate to say, but all we managed to do was mimic an old Bill Cosby routine, where a dead man has a tape recorder in his coffin. As his friends file by, the tape plays, "Why hello, Bob. How's the wife and kids? You're looking well. Don't I look well?"

My relatives were all chain-smoking down the hall, in the mortuary's lounge. I didn't point out that my dad's passion for cigarettes was precisely what earned him this sudden, permanent vacation in Flavor Country.

The viewing room was stuffed with people I was supposed to know. "Come on, you remember Mr. Nameless Pinstripe Suit! He worked with your father at the old office." Oh yeah, him. I was just four years old when Dad worked there, but I'm still embarrassed at my ignorance. My only shot at being the thoughtful daughter of the deceased, and I'm totally blowing it.

I told my uncle Doug that I wanted to be one of the pallbearers. I feel obligated to carry Dad. How many times had he carried me?

In high school I had to dissect a cat that looked a lot like my own. "It's just cells, it's not a cat," I'd whisper to myself with each cut. When I clutched the casket's brass rail, a cold weight shifted inside, and I told myself, "It's just cells, it's not a dad."

We carried him up a small ridge and rested him on the Astroturf surrounding the new grave. I had the sudden thought that my father always preferred playing on natural grass and that he must think it's a shame that all this prime golf course acreage was being squandered on dead people.

Lights Out

STACY, RADIO STATION PROGRAM DIRECTOR, 39

My first dead body was that of Eva Hooter, who was a resident and caretaker of an apartment building where I lived in Cincinnati. I had only been there about six months. Before that I was living in Kentucky and thought I was in a rut—but I was actually just comfortable. When you're twenty-seven, you don't know the difference between rut and comfortable. So I went home to Cincinnati, trying out a new career and hoping to be a new person and seeing where life might take me when I was at home.

Eva was the aunt of the woman who owned the building where I lived. It was a very small building, and all the residents knew each other by name. I was the youngest tenant living there. It was like I moved in with the Golden Girls. Eva was a cross between a mean old lady and a sweet old lady. She would not stand for it if there was loud music coming from any apartment in the building, would not hear of people walking across the grass. You could count on it when you had friends visit that it was Eva's nose poking through the blinds, watching them come across the street. She guarded that building and drove everyone crazy with her "lights on/lights off at a certain time" rule. She really was so particular about the hours when the lights should be turned off and on.

One night I came home from dinner, and the building was pitch dark. I knew something was really, really wrong. I opened the door to the building, and there was Eva on the floor of the foyer, dead. I almost tripped over her. I can still remember: she had jeans on. She was ninety-two and wore jeans all the time with these little flowers embroidered on the back pocket. I remember being transfixed by that. Still, when I think of her dead body, that's what I think of.

She was lying right beneath the light switch. I ran upstairs and knocked on Blanche's door and said, "Blanche, have you heard anything?" And she said, "Well, I think I heard a thump about twenty minutes ago, but I just dismissed it." I looked at her, kind of blinked, and ran into my apartment and dialed 911. The first question from the operator was, "Do you know CPR?" And I was ashamed to admit I didn't. She said, "Well, I'm sending some-body." I ran back downstairs, even though I knew there was noth-ing I could do, even if I had known CPR.

The EMTs arrived, and they tried to comfort me. I was in shock and really quiet and kind of wringing my hands and saying, "If I'd just known CPR, I could have helped." They told me she had been dead for some time and there was absolutely nothing I could have done. They kept saying, "She was ninety-two, had a massive heart attack, and died before she hit the ground." But it upset me so badly that I couldn't sleep that night.

The funeral was a couple days later. When I got there, the mourners consisted of just Blanche, Eva's niece, and me. It just made me so sad. I thought, "Well, maybe when you're ninety-two you outlive everybody." But when my own grandmother died at ninety-two, her funeral was packed. There just weren't that many people there for Eva, and it shocked me and made me so sad for her. I felt this loneliness. I cried and cried. And Eva's niece said to me, "Why are you so upset?" And I said, "I don't know, maybe because I found her and I still felt like there was something I could have done." Somehow I felt responsible.

After the funeral and after I pulled myself together, the first thing I did was sign up for a CPR class, and I started making sure those lights were on at the right time. I took over turning the lights on. I got up on a ladder and replaced the floodlights and swept out the basement and took care of the place. It just knocked me completely out of that twenty-something "all that matters is me" stage of my life. There was something about finding that woman dead and seeing her so friendless at the end of her life that just completely stopped me in my tracks.

Into thin Air

PAULA, PR CONSULTANT, 28

In ninth grade I was on the yearbook staff. I didn't play sports, so it was the one nerdy thing that would give me something to do on the weekends. August was another nerdy kid on the yearbook staff. He was in the eighth grade. I wouldn't say we were total outcasts, but we were definitely not cool kids; I wasn't a cheer-leader, and he wasn't a football player, so we used to hang out together.

Going to yearbook meant going for a three-hour lunch on Sat-urdays and then working on the yearbook for maybe half an hour. It was really a chance to hang out and be out of the house. So Au-gust and I would go to lunch at T.G.I. Friday's on Saturday, under the guise of being on a school-sponsored activity, and we'd sit there over our cheeseburgers and just talk about some pretty pro-found stuff for fourteen- and fifteen-year-olds to talk about.

I remember the last Saturday that I ever saw him; he was talking about his mom and his father. They were Greek, first-generation immigrants, kind of like my parents, except mine are from Hong Kong. We'd complain about our lives together and do our little teenage talking, "my parents did such and such." His mother had gotten some cosmetic surgery procedure on her eyes, and it was a big deal because his father didn't want her to get it. And they'd had this big argument. And that was our big conversation for that Saturday. We went home at three o'clock, and I went back to my little life, and he went back to his little life, and we were like, "Okay, see you on Monday."

Monday morning at school in first period, our teacher, Mr. Russo, walked into the classroom, and he was very serious. He said, "We have an announcement: August died over the weekend in an accident."

I thought he was lying, that it was a big joke. It didn't occur to me that a teacher wouldn't joke about death. The first thing out of my mouth was, "I just saw him on Saturday. How could he be dead?" And for the entire first period I kept saying to myself, "I just saw him two days ago!"

That's why I remembered the conversation so well, because I kept playing it over in my head, like, "Was that real? If he's dead, does that mean he wasn't with me on Saturday?" I couldn't understand the reality of it, that he just was not there anymore. In other words, so he's not going to be there next Saturday? Was he there last Saturday? Was this for real? It was that total disconnect with reality that kind of got to me about the whole death situation. Later on that day, I was like, "Wow, he is dead!" I just remember that the world was kind of going on around me, all the kids were fine, the hallway was as noisy as ever, classes were still being attended. It was like the world didn't stop, August just happened to not be there.

It was the first time that I ever figured out that death was for real. No one had ever died in my family, and no one ever really talked about it. I'd say, "Mom, what happened to your dad?" And she'd say, "Oh yeah, my dad died when I was younger. He died choking on blah, blah, blah." She just told me about the death like it was conversation filler. My mom believes in karma, and she told me that her father died choking on a pork bone. And he was a pig farmer and had to slaughter pigs. She said, "See what happens in life? What you do will always affect how you go."

But you know, it's kind of weird. Nothing really stops. You still go to class, teachers are still telling you to answer questions. And then you go home and you do your homework, and then you go to sleep and you go to school the next day. It's almost like falling in love with my husband. One day we were dating, we were on our first date, and then next thing I knew we were in love and moving in together. It was never like this big staggering realization. With August's death it was the same thing, it was, "Oh, he's dead. He's not here anymore." And then weeks later he's still not around. It became more and more permanent every day.

I didn't go to his funeral. My mom and dad were not the kind of people to whom you could say, "My friend died. I want to go to the funeral." I didn't even tell them he died. I didn't tell anybody. And that was the thing about August and me. We weren't the kind of people who had other people walking up to them in the hallway and saying, "How are you doing?" That's another reason August and I were such good friends—we were cut from the same cloth, we just kind of let things happen.

I don't remember anybody coming up to me other than that first-period teacher, who could see that I was clearly disturbed. Later on that day he saw me in the hallway and was like, "Are you okay?" And he asked me the next day, too. And that was the only recognition I got from anybody that my friend had died. I didn't see anybody else in the hallway talking about it; no one else said anything about it. There were a couple of kids who said, "I heard he fell off this balcony. I wonder if he jumped." Those cruel things that people say.

All of the emotions that go with death, the sense of loss, happened to me. But they happened in a very different way, in a very solitary manner. There wasn't anyone around me that was talking to me about it, so I just worked through it myself. I think at that age no one really knows how to process anything. And I also think that when you're older and wiser, you know that it's okay to cry and say you're sad and be vocal about it. But back then I didn't know. Was I supposed to tell people I was really upset? And if I did, did that mean I was blaming August? What if I failed a test? Was I trying to blame that on his death?

I read an article recently, in *The New York Times Magazine*. The article was written by this guy whose friend had just died. His friend hadn't committed suicide on purpose. He fell off a balcony, too. In the article he says his friend "wasn't the type of guy who would kill himself. He was just the kind of guy who wouldn't think that hanging off the balcony might mean that you might fall off which might mean that you might die."

And I think that's the same thing that happened to August. No one's ever going to know. The details never leaked out, and his parents never made any statements. But I don't think that August was the type of guy who would say, "Gosh, if I jump right now, it's going to be so great! I'm going to kill myself." He was the kind of guy who might have hung off a balcony and said, "Wow, that's really high," and not thought about the consequences.

It was really odd. We were just two nerdy kids. It's not like we were total outcasts like the movies portray, because I think that in real life it's very rare that you get those kinds of nerds that you see in the movies. You just get the ones who no one thinks is cool, the ones who don't get invited to the parties. August and I weren't straight A students; we were just average kids. In school we were just there. Nobody went out of his or her way to make fun of us; nobody went out of the way to include us. In the end, I ended up in New York, and I married, and I'm happy, and things are great. But in the end, he's not.

Sealing the Hole

MARTA, CHILDREN'S BOOK EDITOR, 33

When I was twenty-five, one of my best friends died of AIDS, two weeks before his twenty-fifth birthday. I had been to other funerals, and I had known other people my age who had died. There was a girl in high school killed by a drunk driver, a good friend's boyfriend who had a motorcycle crash and wasn't wearing a helmet, a former carpool friend killed while he was driving drunk. Not to be blasé, but the usual teenage deaths.

I used to teach English 101 at the University of Cincinnati, and one of the assigned themes was "The Most Significant Event of Your Life." This is a very stupid subject to assign to eighteen-year-olds, because most of them write about the prom. But there are always three or four students whose *"best friend"* died in high school. Usually, as you work on the paper with them, you discover that it was not in fact their best friend, but a guy they passed every day in the hall and once said hi to at a party. Teenagers are so naturally melodramatic, they love death. They love tragedy and thinking their lives exist in a moment.

But this was not one of those teenage deaths. This was not a situation where everyone gets together after the funeral and cries prettily and tries to get the cute guys to hug them, then a week later resumes driving while "a little tipsy."

This was me and a group of friends trying to figure out what music to play at the funeral ("Amazing Grace" and Madonna's "Like a Prayer"), trying to figure out how to write a eulogy, trying to figure out what a five-foot-five boy who weighed about ninety pounds at death should be dressed in. Trying to figure out whether to give in to his parents' request for a Catholic service.

I remember thinking that it really sucked that I had to plan a friend's funeral before my mother ever did. That my mother could in no way help me figure out how to get Mark's partner to eat something. How to get myself to eat something without gagging. My mother could not tell me the gracious way to kick an ex-boyfriend of Mark's out of the funeral home before Mark's partner saw him.

My mother could not tell me that it would all be okay, that I would eventually stop crying every time I was left alone for more than five minutes, because she had no way of knowing if that was true or not.

I became the sort of capable neighborhood woman who always knows what kind of casserole to bring (or in our case how many cartons of cigarettes to buy), and it scared and thrilled me. So much of my teenage identity had been built on being precocious and cute. I now knew I could be an adult, a woman, a mother. I think it scared my mother, too. She'd never been very maternal, but this was the first time her daughter was going through something she had no way to offer an opinion on. This was the first time I was clearly more competent and knowledgeable than her.

I have been through the deaths and funerals of other friends since then. But nothing has ever hurt as much as Mark dying, and I don't think it ever will. It is not that I love Mark more than my other friends or my family. It's that his death changed the world for me.

I recently saw the movie *West Side Story*. I remember watching it in high school and thinking that there was no way Maria could ever recover from Tony's death, that she might as well die herself.

When I saw it now, at the age of thirty-three, I thought how silly it was that Tony essentially killed himself because he thought Maria was dead. How silly for her to think this was the biggest tragedy life could offer.

Mark told me once he was glad that Barbie (another friend of ours) and I were his best girlfriends because we'd probably never get married and leave him. For whatever reason, as teens and people in our early twenties, this group all believed that we were the only people on earth who truly loved and understood each other.

A few months ago at my wedding we all spent a moment remembering Mark, then went out on the dance floor to music he would have loved, if he'd lived long enough to hear it created. This weekend at Barbie's wedding we did the same thing.

This is the way in which Mark's death changed the world for me (and broke my heart). It showed me that everything we learn about tragedy and heartache as melodramatic teens is not true. The world *is* unbearably cruel and unfair, but you get over it. Your best friend dies, and it leaves a hole in your heart—but you later discover to your shock, horror, and delight that everyone has holes in their heart, and you still live.